LEGAL TENDER

WOMEN
&
THE SECRET LIFE OF MONEY

Christian McEwen

Bauhan Publishing
Peterborough, New Hampshire
2019

Library of Congress Cataloging-in-Publication Data
Names: McEwen, Christian, 1956- author.
Title: Legal tender : women & the secret life of money / Christian
McEwen.
Description: Peterborough, NH : Bauhan Publishing, [2019] |
Includes bibliographical references.
Identifiers: LCCN 2019010108 | ISBN 9780872332935 (softcover :
alk. paper)
Subjects: LCSH: Women—Finance, Personal. | Women's rights. |
Equality.
Classification: LCC HG179.M3746 2019 | DDC 332.0240082—dc23
LC record available at https://lccn.loc.gov/2019010108

Book design by Henry James and Sarah Bauhan.
Cover Design by Henry James.
Cover art by Annie Bissett with images from her book *Loaded*,
which can be seen on **www.anniebissett.com**
Author photo by Joanna Eldredge Morrissey

To contact Christian McEwen, visit **www.christianmcewen.com**

BAUHAN
PUBLISHINGLLC
PO BOX 117 PETERBOROUGH NEW HAMPSHIRE 03458

WWW.BAUHANPUBLISHING.COM

Follow us on Facebook and Twitter – @bauhanpub

MANUFACTURED IN THE UNITED STATES OF AMERICA

LEGAL
TENDER

If "money talks," it is with our voice.

—Lynne Twist

In memory of Ann Stokes,
Quaker philanthropist—

her generosity & rebel spirit

CONTENTS

FOREWORD

SEVERAL YEARS AGO Christian McEwen interviewed me about my relationship to money. As the self-proclaimed "Chief Inspiration Officer" of the women's funding community, I have spent decades facilitating conversations on this subject, both in women's groups and in the larger philanthropic community, encouraging everyone to give and to invest in accordance with their deepest values.

But it wasn't easy, even for me, to face the truth of my own money story. In that first conversation with Christian, I shared my life story and I came out. Not as a cancer survivor. Not as a person who doesn't appear to need open heart surgery. Not as the daughter of an alcoholic with mental illness. Not even as a lesbian feminist—been there, done that. All those identities were easier to claim than the facts of my relationship to money. Coming out about money is scary and real.

When Christian asked me what class I had been raised in, I paused—then told her I'd been born into a class of hard knocks, and now live in a class of comfort and elegance. Some people call those classes "working poor" and "middle class." I prefer to name them for what they are—one a class with multiple daily challenges and limits, and one whose days brim full with many gorgeous choices. My money story is a blend of hard knocks, hard work, good luck, and (now) much-appreciated ease and grace.

In the years since, I have had the opportunity to share my story many times, both privately and from the podium. I have also had the pleasure of working with Christian through the Jewish Women's Funding Network, using some of the stories included here. Whether she read the stories herself or they were performed by a professional actor didn't seem to matter—the audience was immediately transformed. Everyone was eager to share money stories of their own. Lively conversation, ease, and laughter filled the room, accompanied by an almost palpable sense of relief. I was struck by the power of such stories to reveal people to themselves, uncovering old wounds, and giving form and clarity to what has long been an anonymous ache.

As the Money and Power Fellow for the Women's Funding Network and the founder of Imagine Philanthropy, my life has been committed to the ideals of "equal say" for women in leadership, and "equal play and pay" in sports and money. Unconscious or implicit biases around gender have kept women out of most leadership positions, especially in the financial arena (ranging from home to leadership to venture capital). Now, as more people become aware of the challenges (and toxicity!) of living under "the rule of fathers," we are ever more hungry to hear women's testimony. Sharing our individual money stories can be deeply healing and liberating, allowing us to be vulnerable and powerful at the same time.

Recent research by the Women's Philanthropic Institute shows that as women become bolder with our money, we gain courage, confidence, and control. Courage to take risks and try new things. Confidence to speak up about how we use our money, and delight in being in control of it.

Women build bridges, we forge peace, we build community infrastructure, we break down barriers, we speak for those who have no voice, we stop corruption, we transform the world. To do this well and thrive, we must share our stories, own our power, control our resources and, increasingly, deploy them with a gender lens.

Read on to learn how Christian helps bring these powerful stories and the art of storytelling to all of us in an accessible way. Find yourself in *Legal Tender: Women & the Secret Life of Money* and allow your own story to reveal itself to you. Our world depends on it.

In sisterhood,
Tuti B. Scott

Founder and President, *Imagine Philanthropy*

INTRODUCTION

*Everyone has to make up their mind if money is money
or money isn't money and sooner or later they always do
decide that money is money.*

—Gertrude Stein

A T SIX YEARS OLD, I was given my first pocket money:
two big brown pennies for each year of my life, which
is to say, one old-fashioned silver shilling every week
(worth, in those days, about fifteen cents). It wasn't a lot
of money even then. I remember harboring an enormous
lust for cash. Christmas and birthdays sometimes brought
checks, or what were called premium bonds. My sister and
I competed with one another: *Who had the more generous
godparents?*

In *Mary Poppins*, Mr. Banks goes to the City and sits at a
large desk cutting out pennies and shillings and half-crowns
and threepenny bits, which he brings home with him in a little black bag. That was about my level of understanding too. I
had no expectation of competence or practicality. I was told
from early on: "None of the McEwens are any good with

numbers." I remember a perpetual fizz of adult anxiety about school fees and taxes and the latest heating bill, along with a rueful little jingle that my father liked to repeat:

> *That money talks, I won't deny,*
> *I heard it once, it said, "Good-bye!"*

As I grew up and moved out into the world, I held firm to one aim only: *not to get into debt, not to live beyond my (very modest) means.* My father died, too young, at fifty-three. Not long afterwards, my mother was declared bankrupt. There were innumerable family dramas. Far away in the United States, I did what I could to keep a roof over my head. I had the financial skills of an earnest eight-year-old, able to add and subtract, but only barely to calculate a tip. For years, I maintained a kind of mild, old-fashioned probity. I had no credit card debt—but, of course, no credit either. Still, I did manage, though in a strange, cramped way, buttressed by considerable ignorance, bewilderment, terror, and self-blame. And in this, I realize, I was not alone.

⤺

I have been thinking about women and money for more than a decade, starting in the spring of 2009. In that time, I've interviewed more than fifty women about their relationship to money, resulting in a play called *Legal Tender*, and its sister project, a book of money stories, which you now hold in your hands. Those I spoke to came from a wide range of racial and ethnic backgrounds—English, Irish, Polish, and African American; Jewish, Italian, Portuguese, and Puerto Rican—and many more besides. Some had grown up in the comfortable reaches of the upper and upper middle classes. Others described themselves as middle class, or self-made working class. There were those who'd inherited big money from their families, and others who'd had to scrimp and save for every penny. But whatever their circumstances, what struck me was how often these women were telling stories they had never told before, or not in any coherent or sequential way.

I came up with a list of questions, and though I tweaked them a little, basically I asked everyone the same few crucial things: *What did you learn about money growing up? How did your parents deal with it? Were you raised to feel competent in financial terms? What was your first job?* Then I worked over the transcriptions with a fine-tooth comb, pulling out the liveliest and most surprising stories, adding choruses and quotes, and braiding them together to create this book.

The text that follows can be read from start to finish, or picked up and browsed at intervals. Because of the way it is organized, it can also be used in a class on financial literacy, women's studies, or personal memoir, focusing in turn on one specific theme (childhood, gender studies, inheritance, etc.) and using that as catalyst for writing or discussion. Best of all, perhaps, is to explore the different stories by reading them aloud, coming up with a favorite selection of your own, and carrying that out into the larger community.

Back in 2014, a group of us were able to do exactly that for a local audience in Northampton, Massachusetts. An all-female cast (some skilled professional actors, some utter novices) read the work aloud, backed by a swaying curtain of dollar bills. Each sold-out performance played to a full house, there was front-page coverage in the local newspaper, and for several enchanted weeks it seemed that everyone I knew was trading money stories with their friends and family.

↞

The word *money* derives from Moneta, the Roman goddess of abundance and fertility, and is linked to an Indo-European root meaning "to think or use one's mind," and thence to Mnemosyne, the Greek goddess of memory. I find myself delighted by this little knot of associations, as if talking about money—making sense of it—*remembering the stories*—were itself a source of possible riches.

As women's money stories are more widely shared, we get to learn from one another: to witness someone else's liberality and expertise, and to be inspired by it. Clearly, generosity itself is often generative. But I would argue that *honesty* and *openness* are crucial too, banishing the shame and ignorance from which so many of us have suffered, drawing us forward into a new place of ease and self-forgiveness, and, if we are lucky, providing clarity and company along the way. Hence this little book of money stories, with its emphasis on *listening, asking questions*, its confidence that each person's courage, accuracy, and authenticity can help to liberate us all. *Legal tender, legal tenderness.*

May we all make time to hear each other's stories.

The Money

The money I spent traveling
round these dis-United States

The loose bills
in the ladies' room at Central Park

The check that arrived
astonishingly in the mail

My mother's money
in its small red leather purse

The farthings
I collected as a child

The two gold sovereigns
that my father bought for me

The money someone owes me
that will never be repaid

The silver coin
my friend keeps in her shoe,

to walk, she says,
towards prosperity

The money
That I just don't have right now

The money to buy poetry
and sweet, old-fashioned roses

to pay for laughter, peace of mind,
serenity

That money....

CHILDHOOD

"**P**APA! WHAT'S MONEY?" asks the small Paul Dombey, in the novel by Charles Dickens. In the first section of this book, women reach back to childhood to come up with answers of their own. There is the confusion when money seems to multiply all by itself. "Mommy, how did that happen? She gave you back so many! You just gave her one!" There is the anxiety about how best to spend it, and the effort to earn or save it, somehow to make sense of what it means.

It is clear, even from the first two stories (focusing on Esther, the "Girl Gambler," and a young African American student called Charisma), that the subject is not going to be an easy one. "Most people would rather tell you about blow-jobs they gave to strangers on the highway than talk about money honestly," Esther says forthrightly. She sees herself as a rare exception. "I'm not embarrassed by money. I'm not embarrassed by having it or not having it."

Charisma, on the other hand, who grew up with an absent father and a mother on disability, has acute memories of deprivation. "I wouldn't fully call it 'shame,'" she says, doing her valiant best to transform her complicated feelings into something more socially acceptable. And later, awkwardly, as she starts to work, and crashes headlong into debts and credit cards and extra fees, "I guess for me, in my situation, I just learned through making my mistakes."

⸺

The Language of Money

Bread, blunt, dough, moolah.
Dosh, loot, jack, rhino.
Bawbees, spondoolies, mopus, dust.

Salt, chink, oof, brass.
The readies.
Pin money, pocket money, cold hard cash.

Esther: The Girl Gambler

MOST PEOPLE WOULD RATHER tell you about blow-jobs they gave to strangers on the highway than talk about money honestly. I think it's because it's so random. I know what a healthy relationship to sex is. I just don't know about a healthy relationship to money! When you're rich, you can pretend it means something about you personally. And when you're not, you want to believe it has nothing to do with who you are. . . .

I'm not embarrassed by money. I'm not embarrassed

by having it, or not having it. When a man takes a wad of money out of his pocket, his shoulders are back, he's strong and confident. When women do it *[she hunches over protectively]* they're like this. They're embarrassed by money. I don't know where that comes from, but I do notice it: women get totally crazy. And I'm never jealous of other people's money. I have a friend who's fairly wealthy—she's never worried about money one second in her life. She's lost two husbands, she's had cancer twice, she's had a double mastectomy, and people say to me, "Look at her, she's so lucky!" And I go—*Wow!!*

⤶

My name is Esther. I'm a worker, yeah, and solidly middle class. I had a CPA for a father and a bookkeeper for a mother. But what I learned was "easy come, easy go." There was respect for people in our house, but absolutely no respect for money. I try not to be like that. I fight it, you know? But I've never had savings in my whole entire life. My husband's an artist. He makes wood furniture and metal sculpture, and his business is the great sinkhole, so whatever money we have goes into that.

When I was eight or nine I went to the tracks for the first time with my father and my uncles. It was this incredible world. These sexy gorgeous women and real crazy men. Everybody had a story and a nickname, and I just loved it there. They taught me how to read the racing form, which was like learning Greek. My boy cousins couldn't understand it, but I got it! I started to say, "Well, it's raining tonight and this horse has never won in the rain. But look at this one, this long shot, this horse has run in the rain five times." And I would say to my father, "What about this one? Why don't you bet on this one?" And you know, I'm obsessive. I was an obsessive five-year-old! I loved the track and I loved going with them and I started to do really well. I would pick a race a night usually, and they'd give me money and let me bet on it by myself and I'd share in the winnings, and it was just so heady and fabulous. We'd have prime rib dinners and the men would have a couple of shots of whiskey, and everybody smoked and you could smell that. My clothes stank and I loved it! And then at the end they'd hand me thirty bucks. I was a kid. Thirty bucks was a fortune!

I remember buying this transistor radio that cost, like, sixty dollars. I'd been eyeing it for weeks. And the man goes, "Where did you get that money?" I said "It's mine! It's mine!" So, I liked every part of it.

I'm thinking about poker all the time, and the rest of my life—work, family, friends—seems like filler.

—Martha Frankel

When I first met my husband, Rob, I used to bet on horses all the time. And then I got into football and I started betting on the games. I was really good at it. One night we were at the bar and I was betting on something and Rob said, "You know, this really makes me uncomfortable." 'Cause his family had never gambled. So I put the books away and didn't do it. Didn't gamble for many, many years.

Years later, I went down to Florida and my cousin Keith taught me how to play poker. He took me to the casino where his wife worked, and I did great. It was like being a kid again, 'cause it's all about numbers and percentages. Plus reading people is part of my job. So the poker table was like one big happy family, and I was really good at it. Then I came home and my best friend's husband played in a poker game, and I asked if I could join. I wound up winning that first night, and I thought, *Oh, I could be good at this!* And then I just became obsessed, and I taught myself to play and play and play and play. And I played in casinos when I went to LA. I drove to Atlantic City a few times, and I started getting better and better, and winning more and more.

Then somebody told me about online poker, and *how great is that?!!* You don't even have to leave the house. You can stay home in your pajamas. So I started doing that, and I lost three hundred dollars the first night. And I threw up! I thought I was going to die! I was so embarrassed and freaked out. I said, "Oh my God, I'll never do that again!"

And then I lost three hundred dollars the next day and the next day. . . . The thing about being an addict is you believe you cannot stop. You say, "Okay, tomorrow, first of the month . . ." Every addict does that. My addiction was just like throwing money away. I lost more than my house cost me. Probably seventy-five thousand dollars! I kept at it for a year and a half. But yeah, it was crazy! Every day was like torture. I woke up every day and was completely freaked out.

Then one day, I just couldn't do it. I couldn't lie and hide and cheat one moment more. It took me a long time to pay back the money, but I did, and the burden was on me and nobody else. I've known lots of men who've killed themselves because the gambling debts got so out of control. Every month you don't pay the thing, it just multiplies and, *oh my God!* It's just horrible, horrible. Even after I stopped, that didn't end the money hole that I was in. So I never slept. I was completely paranoid someone would find out.

And then one day I thought maybe if I wrote about it, it would be over. Get it out of my system. I thought I was going to write this happy, snappy little book about poker and my family. Then I met an agent and I told her how I had gambled online and lost tens of thousands of dollars, and she said, "Oh, I could sell *that!*"

Rob knew nothing about those losses—I kept them hidden from everyone—until the book was written and at my publisher's, and I finally had to give it to him. That was just horrible. I mean, he's a really honest, down-to-earth, hard-working, lovely man. And every part of me had been lying to him. And I had to show it to my sister and my brother-in-law and the people I love, and say, "Okay, this is who I am. I'm a liar and a cheat and an addict. And not only that, but I want you to still love me and forgive me." Nobody let me down.

Absolutely nobody. To me it is a miracle, my own private miracle, that my friends and family still love me. I'm a very judgmental person, and I'm not sure how I would have reacted. I'm not sure I wouldn't have . . . banished me. But nobody did.

And you know what? I am such a better person for having done this. People ask, "Don't you wish you had never done it?" And I say, "Oh no. No, no, no!" Not that I would recommend it, but I'm not sorry. I learned so much about myself and the people I love. And that I put my faith in the right ones.

I'm so grateful I stopped when I did. I could so easily have done something really stupid, 'cause you know, bookmakers love an addictive gambler. They love us. And now people ask, "Well, are you going to do it again?" And I say, "Nah. I'm so over it." That doesn't mean I'm not capable of getting obsessed by something else. I hear from a lot of gamblers who tell me, "I can't stop." And I say, "Yes, you can, and you will. One day you will."

↵

I've been rich and I've been poor. Rich is better.
—Sophie Tucker

Charisma: Not Shame, Exactly

MY NAME IS CHARISMA. And I'm twenty-one years old. I'd put myself in . . . the working class. My mom injured herself while she was pregnant with me. She had to go on disability. So we were on government assistance. And she's been on assistance ever since.

My dad was in the picture until I was six. He'd go to work every day—supply—for the family. Then he got kicked out, for drugs and alcohol. I'd say from the stories I've heard, that if my mom asked for money, my dad would give it to her. Without any questions. So, you could say my mom made the financial decisions, and he just supplied. For the most part, she would be the Regulator.

Being on government assistance, and my mom having a lot of children—sometimes we didn't have food in our house. 'Cause you get paid once a month, and you have to make that last. Sometimes we wouldn't have, like, full cooked meals at night. I'd have to make sure to eat at school. All of us got free lunch.

And I did feel, you know, sometimes, left out, when my friends wanted to go out. Especially my best friend, she always wanted to go out, and I'd have to tell her, "No, I don't have any money." And then she was like, "Well, I'll just pay for you." And I'd go out, but at the same time, it's just—it's not my own, something that I can, you know, be proud of spending.

I wouldn't fully call it "shame." I have this weird thing where, as I go through, I guess, obstacles and hardships, I turn it into determination and motivation.

It's disappointing as a child. But you just get over it. I wouldn't feel like, I can't walk the streets, they can't see me like this, you know. Like, It's okay. It happens.

↲

At a certain point, my mom would say, "You think you're grown now. And since you're grown, you need to find a job!" And I was like, "I can't find a job. I'm in high school, and I'm in this extra program that's helping me get to college, and I don't have time for it, you know." But I finally got a job at the age of eighteen, working at Macy's. We got paid weekly, which I thought was just awesome. Eight dollars an hour. But once you see those taxes come out, you're like, "Oh! I work so hard for pennies!"

Basically I do whatever I want with my money, whether it's buying food to give me comfort, or buying food because there is no food, or just buying things to make me feel happy. Just to feel like I'm a teenager. 'Cause I grew up too fast, you know.

I remember seventh grade. Seventh or eighth grade? My math teacher. She taught us about your checks and your balances. But how're we going to know about that if we don't have a bank account? How's that going to play out when you finally have a credit card, and you think that's just awesome, I have a credit card! And then you realize, I shouldn't have bought that. And you regret it. You get in debt. Or you're charged extra fees . . .

I guess for me, in my situation, I just learned through making my mistakes.

↩

My family comes from Saint Thomas, US Virgin Islands. Before we were conquered by the United States, we were conquered by the Danish. We were former slaves. And even though we fought back against the Danish, and the United States became our savior, basically the message was: "You're inferior." It's not like we can take pride in being black.

But the funny thing is that I'd say my grandmother is— middle class? Working middle class. More towards middle class than working class. She owns a house. She has titles. But most of her children didn't turn out the way she turned out.

So it's more than just an American thing. It's the class issue, it's the race issue, and then it's the gender issue, because of course the parents are more lenient with the boys. It's like, "It's okay for you to mess up. It's okay for you to make mistakes." But with the women, it's, "No, that was very wrong. You shouldn't have done that. You just ruined your whole life." But it's not ruined, you know. *Why did you treat me differently than my brother?*

So, everything's just tied together—in one big clump.

↩

My mom took my father to court for child support, but from the age—Lord knows! I'd say from twelve or thirteen, I didn't see any of it. Then, one time I had a conversation with my father, and he's like, "So you're not getting the child support that's coming out of my check?!!" And I'm like, "Well, no! I don't see any money." He's like, "Well, your mother's keeping it." And I'm like, "Is that so? Because she says she's not getting anything." So! Come to find out she *was*. And she felt that she was obligated to take the money that's for me, for her.

She said, "I spent it on food! Things that you need!" And I don't know if that's true or not. I don't think it will ever be explained! It's always going to be, "Well, I'm your mother, and I deserve this." So who knows?

Each week I calculate how much I'm getting paid. And then I take out ten or twenty dollars, 'cause that's you know, taxes. I write a list of things I have to pay off, and a list of things I might want to get, and then, as soon as Friday comes—it's all gone! It's all gone, because I'm paying off everything.

Most of the time my money goes to food, outside food. 'Cause the college spoils me. It gives me three meals a day. So when you don't have three meals a day sitting in front of you, you're like, "Maybe I should go get just one sandwich." And then one sandwich turns into three sandwiches for three meals. So it's like, "Oh, my money's gone for today! Well, what are we going to eat tomorrow?"

❧

With Letty, oh dear! I walked into her office, bawling, crying, because I couldn't pay my college bill. The Financial Aid Office wouldn't budge, wouldn't smile, just kept a straight face and said, "You need to pay this, or you'll have to leave." And I went to the president's office, and the assistant to the president was really rude, and basically asked me why am I here. And I felt it was because of my race.

So I went to Letty's office, and I'm crying, telling her my whole story, how my mom doesn't help me, and my dad's not in the picture, hasn't helped for quite a while, and I'm like, "I don't know what to do!" They're taking twenty-four dollars out of my check, and I only get paid eighty dollars a week. There's no way I could survive.

And Letty was just like, "I'll write you a check." And I said, "What?" And she's like, "Yes, I'll write you a check." And I felt like I probably—kept crying.

'Cause this was just amazing. And she was like, "I saw something in you, " and how she knows that this is the right place for me, where I can grow. She's like, "I'ma help you out. And I know one day you're going to help someone else out, when they need it." And I was like, "You are so right."

How much was it? Oh, my God! Lord take the wheel! So my first year—oh, that's plus health insurance. So I would say eight, no, more than—six to nine thousand?

&

For every $100 of wealth in white families, families of color have just $5.04.
—Census Bureau Current Population Survey, reported in *The New York Times*, September 2017.

How It Grows

AS A CHILD, I REMEMBER going into a store with my mother, and she handed the lady one piece of money, and the lady handed her back several. And I was astounded. "Mommy, how did that happen? She gave you back so many! You just gave her one!" And I guess that's my basic notion about money.

Necco Wafers

MY AUNT WOULD SIT DOWN with my brother and me when we were very small, and she would open her change purse and say, "You may count the pennies and divide them between you." And that generally preceded something she called "an apple party," which meant using a very pretty dish and a very pretty knife and cutting an apple in sections so we could eat it.

I was given an allowance of ten cents a week. We went to a little mom-and-pop store on the shore of the lake. And you had a choice to make with your ten cents. You could get a pack of lemon drops, a package of peppermints, a Hershey bar (with or without almonds), or Necco wafers, all different flavors. The thing about Necco wafers was there were flavors you couldn't stand, so you had to go with a friend so you could trade off: "If you take the black ones, I'll take the red ones," and you'd work it out.

And that was a heavy decision.

Hey, Lady!

SO, OVER THANKSGIVING, we're having this family discussion. And the nieces and nephews are saying, "How old were you when you started working?" And Pat and I say, "We were about nine." And they say, "No way!" So I ask my brother, who's two years younger than me, "Tom! How old were you when you started working?" He says, "I think I was eight." I ask him, "What were we doing, Tom?" And he says, "You kidding? We were all over the place doing whatever anybody needed. So, 'Hey, lady, you want the snow shoveled? Hey, lady, you want the leaves raked?' You know, we would just go all over doing stuff." And it was hard to get in trouble 'cause we all looked alike!

↢

The Saver

AS A CHILD, I WAS THE SAVER. The hoarder of money, and the hider of money. I learned that saving was really important, but—oh, so hard to do! Because emergencies would come up all the time. Like with my brother, who isn't much older than me. We took a family trip to Disney World, we each had our little savings, and my brother spent all his at the airport when we got to, like, Orlando. So I ended up giving him a portion of mine.

That's just the way I was raised. Like, it's what you do, you know. I wasn't resentful in the moment, until, maybe, my money was all gone. Then I'd be like, *"Waugghh!"*

I've had experiences like that in adult life, where I've helped out a family member, and felt guilty about having to hit that person up. Like, "Hey! Can you get me that money now?" And still not having seen the follow-through.

But then I pick up an extra shift. Or count the change I saved. Or search my room 'cause I just know I've hidden a twenty-dollar bill somewhere.

↞

The Proud Way to Be

THIS IS ANOTHER STORY . . . I'm sure nobody else will have a story like this. Third grade, I've just come from China, middle of the year, first time ever in a school. I'm standing in line with the other third graders, and everybody's boasting, about "My father this," and "My parents that." And I'm thinking, What can I say that's going to impress them? And I say, "Well, we're *poor!*"

Dead silence! It's like, What did I say? Why don't they think that's wonderful? I thought that was really the proud way to be.

↞

Teaneck

MY FATHER WAS FAMOUS for doing without. It was always a joke—and I think not untypical of Jewish men of that generation—that they would have nothing for themselves, and be pleased. You know, no golf clubs. They worked. My father worked. He loved music too, and he loved his family. But he worked and he recovered from working, and that was his way.

When I was in third grade, we moved from Palisades Park to Teaneck [New Jersey], which was almost entirely a Jewish town. And Teaneck was a huge change. I remember a kid asking me, "How much property does your father have?" I didn't know what property was! *Property!* It sounded like a tool! "He had ten properties in his workshop!"

Teaneck was a place where women wore *mink* stoles to Rosh Hashanah. In September, mink! I hated it right away. I was an early refusenik.

I ALWAYS WANTED . . .

"**M**ONEY IS ONE OF THOSE HUMAN CREATIONS that makes concrete a sensation," writes Jamie Buchan, "in this case the sensation of wanting, as a clock does the sensation of passing time." As women address their early memories of money, other linked subjects are drawn up into the light, among them race and class and ethnicity, justice and injustice, a tremendous undertow of longing. "It's not fair," wails the child's cry, back across the decades, yearning for a bicycle, a pair of Mary Janes, "a boatload of new turtlenecks," a horse.   The first two stories in this section center on Bridie -- one of many children in a large Irish-American family -- and Ziporah, who describes herself as "Bohemian money-free middle class. A poet. A working artist." Neither woman has ever had much money. But in some essential way, this has not impeded them. As a child, Bridie wanted to be an artist and a writer; she wanted to be a dancer "really bad." Her mother discouraged her. "Get those high-falutin ideas out of your head. Those are for rich kids!" But she also told her, "If you work hard enough, you can get anything you want."

I Always Wanted

I REALLY WANTED A HORSE.

I remember my parents saying, "We don't have a barn."

Somehow I got it into my head that if we had a proper barn, then I could have a horse.

So I got two pieces of wood, and some logs. . . .

I guess it became clear before long this wasn't going to turn into a barn!

I do remember my roommate coming home with, like, a boatload of new turtlenecks and sweaters. Her whole wardrobe changed over Christmas. I got one piece of clothing, maybe. And I was like, *Wow!* Like, *How does she get that?*

If I had money, I'd buy me a nice house.

After you have a house, you want a nice car,

and after a nice car, you want nice furniture, nice clothing.

Like anyone who lives comfortably, like anyone would want.

Who don't want that?

First Jobs

MY FIRST JOB WAS BABYSITTING, which is just so typical of girls.

I think I charged six dollars an hour.

I was twelve years old. I picked strawberries! We got a quarter a quart.

Girl Scout cookies! Lemonade stand!

A summer job with a sailing school.

Hand-coloring old maps for a bookstore.

Ah, teaching tennis. I was a tomboy!

I never had a day job. What can I say? I'm not ambitious.

↩

Bridie: 100% Irish

MY NAME IS BRIDIE, and I'm 100% Irish.

My father grew up like *Angela's Ashes*—did you read that book? That kind of poverty. His dad died, and he was the oldest of three kids. He went out to work when he was six, delivering groceries. And my grandmother scrubbed the marble steps in banks. Somebody in the office would give her the Sunday paper, and that was a big deal; the kids would get to read the funnies, and then they would make thicknesses and cut out soles for their shoes. Every week, they had to put new soles in.

My dad always used to tell us how wonderful newspapers were. You can put them in your coat, for warmth. If a baby's about to be born, newspaper's the cleanest thing to spread around. You can use it to wash windows too, of course. You can use it for a mattress.

He didn't talk a lot about those early years. But my mother

did. So we kinda knew that Daddy grew up poor. And that we were not poor, and that Daddy was going to make sure we were not, even if he had to work three jobs—and he did. He was a fireman and he did construction work, he moonlighted as a cop. Mom said he slept five hours a night. He's, in my family, very revered. You'll hear aunts, uncles, cousins, say, "Your dad! He was the best!" 'Cause he helped so many people. Yeah.

§

I came home from school, I was eight or nine. And the kids had been teasing me and taunting me. You know, they'd call the Irish "ragpickers" or "dirty Mick," things like that, that you usually brushed off. But I guess on this one day I was upset. And I said, "Ma, Ma, are we poor?" And her answer, absolutely spontaneous, was, "*Certainly not!* How could we *possibly* be poor with such a large family?"

My grandfather's saying was, "If you're ever feeling poor or down-on-your-luck, give something away, help somebody else, and you'll feel rich. You'll be a rich person indeed!" And I can remember when we were growing up there was always enough to help other people. *Always!*

Like I remember once, my mother sitting us down and talking about Father Matthew, who had an orphanage in Alabama with all these little children, and they were having a hard year. And so, could we all, as a family, cut back on our Christmas? Now, mind you, *we did not get big gifts for Christmas!* We got little things. But would we all mind cutting back and not having so many presents, meaning not three, only one or something. I can't remember what we got—but it would be, socks, you know.

And we all thought that was a fine idea.

Did I want anything? I don't know. When there's that many kids, you're in a *line of kids,* to get things. So it's pretty hard to have a private thing that's yours. Although I remember winning a doll once, and that was mine. And when I wanted a bike, my dad got me a bike from one of the other firemen's kids. It was a used bike. But it was a bike.

You know how people say, "What do you want to be when you grow up?" I used to say, "I want to be an artist. I want to be a writer. I want to be a dancer." I wanted to be a dancer really bad. And my mom would say, "Get those highfalutin ideas out of your head! Those are for *rich* kids! You kids are going to have to work for everything you've got in this life." And that was, like, *drummed into us.*

But it was also drummed in, "If you work hard enough, you can get anything you want."

⤶

I always said to my kids, "When you graduate from high school, you're on your own. And it's time for me to do something wild and crazy."

When the youngest one graduated, I was working for Franklin County Home Care. I had this solid job. I had health insurance for the first time. And my son said, "Well, are you going to quit?" And I said, "Maybe I should stay on for another year, and

41

make sure everybody's okay." "Ma, you're copping out!"

So, I quit my job. I went to the outdoor leadership program. It was a turning point in my life. I could have stayed in my job and been upwardly mobile for the first time—actually bought new furniture. But I said, "I have my choices." And I very clearly made the choice toward: *What did I want to do when I was nineteen? What were my dreams? What got sidelined?*

And of course I'd never traveled. So I wound up leading canoe trips. 'Cause you always think in those terms: *What do I want to do? I want to travel. How can I get a job, so I can travel?* That's how you do it. And I became a park ranger 'cause I didn't want to see the cities. I wanted to live in beautiful places. And I got to do that.

So I never made choices based on money. I never have, and I still don't. And I never had to worry either. I've been really fortunate.

And I think I've *received* generosity my whole life. Seems like every single day I come home, there are presents on the porch, or on the stairs. *"I made this for you. I had extra of this. I'm moving this."*

And then I had this windfall. My mom died, the tree fell on the house, I broke my ankle. Two months later, a thousand dollars comes in the mail. I open this envelope. It's in cash! Fifty-dollar bills! And I start counting it. *Holy cow!* There's a thousand bucks here. It's anonymous. *"Heard you were having a hard time, hope this eases your way. Happy St. Patrick's Day!"* I asked Will if it was him, and he denies this. I think it might be.

I don't know. But I decided—*I like better not knowing!* 'Cause I get to suspect everyone.

Somebody's house burnt down, and someone else—I don't know if it was cancer or what. So instead of my usual giving ten or fifteen or twenty dollars, I got to drop a hundred bucks in their can. You know! And still had all this money left. And I bought my washing machine.

Sometimes you have to wait a while, but the money comes. I absolutely believe it comes. That's been my experience.

↞

Jo March: "I hate money."
                    —Louisa May Alcott, *Little Women*

Ziporah: Pouf & Sink

HOW WOULD I DEFINE MYSELF? Bohemian money-free middle class. A poet. A working artist. When I moved to the commune, my hope was to live almost without money. In those days, if somebody bought a pair of socks, everybody would look at the socks and make much of them. And I imagined we would all protect each other, and we did.

But after Michael left, and you know there were two children, I really had to learn how to provide. To learn to negotiate how to buy a used car, just go in and wrangle. And I got in touch with a family planner to figure out how to hold on to what money I had. I drew a circle on the map of how far I could travel—where I had day care—and I became one of the most active working artists in the state. And I earned money. I earned, in those days, a lot of money for an artist. I ran myself ragged doing it, but I provided. And I was very proud of that. But the greatest joys of my life, from the outside in and from the inside out, have nothing much to do with money.

↩

My family was in the garment business. So you should be a thrifty shopper, but never stint on quality. The messages never had to do with money per se. They had to do with seemliness and unseemliness. Ostentation of any kind was reprehensible. But schlumpiness and lack of care were just as bad.

We used to joke that my father was "The Word" and my mother was "The Word Revealed." They were serious people, but very amiable and in sync with each other. They had a serious mission: raising the family out of poverty, insecurity, illness, and death, to create utter safety and security, and they had every reason to be proud of it. I must have been given an allowance and encouraged to save it, but I almost never spent money. It wasn't very real to me. I just really thought about what I could do without, rather than how much I could acquire.

My first job was a typist at Hart & Company; they were a plastics concern. I had to type "I am sure you will welcome our entrance into the independent automotive aftermarket." I didn't know how to touch-type, and there was no computer, so I typed "independent automotive aftermarket" over and over again. That was the mats—plastic mats, that they put on the floors, or anything else that gets stuck in a car after it's manufactured. My parents couldn't understand why somebody would sacrifice security and the opportunities that they would have died for, to go do shit work just to be independent, but they sort of admired the ruggedness of it.

I believe I got fifty-four dollars every paycheck.

🍖

I think everybody who works in the freelance world has an inner bag lady who is ready to haunt her. But I haven't had to be that person so far—except in my heart. Today is brought to me by the fact that I have paid my taxes. By the fact that I have paid my mortgage, by the fact that I paid for the wood that's in the stove and the box of tea that produced my tea bag, the Kleenex on the counter and the computer I type on, and that I pay the phone bill, and etc., etc., etc. Those are the building blocks of my playground.

I don't really spend much in any discretionary way, because *why start?* I could find I have a genius for extravagance, and then could be let down and disappointed so much of the time. And I know how to save money, I do. My rainy day fund is adequate for . . . small emergencies.

But one time, the day after Michael and I broke up, I went and bought a brand new bed. It was a hilarious and so tender experience. Nobody was in the store except for Joe, who must have been a thirtysomething African American guy,

45

sort of round, like "good for selling mattresses." And Joe said I could lie down on their sleep analyzer, which was a huge, black, marshmallowy-type thing covered with Naugahyde. And I had to say my name and how tall I was and how much I weighed and what position I slept in and what position my partner, if I had one, slept in, and I just blurted out to Joe, "Well, I'm getting a divorce, well, I'm not married, but I'm . . ." And he said, "It's okay, Ziporah. You just lie on the couch."

And then it showed me I was meant to have a very soft mattress. Every batch of firmness had its own special color, and mine was in the gold section. So he started showing me these different beds and I had to lie down on all of them to see which one would serve. And so I was lying on a bed that was, you know, pushing eight hundred dollars! And then there was tax and a special mattress cover . . . so I was channeling my uncles: "Well, what's the best price you can give me on this? I imagine there's some leeway." So Joe said he could probably chop off the tax and could throw in the mattress pad, and take away my old bed, and there'd be free delivery, and, and—I just said "Okay, Joe, I'm going to do it." I flipped out my Visa card and signed up for it. And he said, "You'll be glad you've done this. With mattresses it's all about pouf and sink." And I said, "Joe, you're talking my language."

The mattress came on New Year's Eve. I'd gone upstairs that morning and I saw how cobwebs had formed all around the room, how my bedroom had become a sad place. So I took down all of the old photographs of the life I had loved so much, and put up photographs of the children. And I loving-ly cleaned my room. After I finished vacuuming and washing things down, I polished all my furniture with oil and vinegar. I'd looked on the Internet to see how to make furniture polish out of things you already have in the house, and apparently you could make an oil and vinegar furniture polish. So I rear-ranged things and just sort of polished away the tears. But my room smelled a little like a salad.

And then the delivery guys threw out the old bed and set up the new one. I made it up with fresh linens and then I started to make friends with the bed of solitude. Or maybe I should call it the bed of gratitude. That I was just able to say, "I must do this now. I must have heart's ease. I must cradle my back."

So when I get into that bed—onto that mattress—with my hot water bottle and the memory-foam pillow they threw in for free, I just think, pouf and sink.

Pouf and sink.

Party Shoes

WHEN I WAS THREE, I knew this little girl called Wendy. And she had a closet full of gorgeous shoes. Party shoes, what we called Mary Janes, all lined up in a long row. It was one thing to have a pair of black Mary Janes. I had a pair, every girl did. But Wendy had red. And yellow and white, and green and pink and purple, all the colors of the rainbow.

So I went to my mother, and I begged her to get me some more shoes. I nagged at her all week: "Oh, Mommy, please!" And of course she told me we could not afford them. "Oh, Mommy, it's not fair! Wendy's so lucky!"

And then my mother laughed, and made a special kind of face. "Well," she said, "her father's a shoe salesman." And she began to explain how much better it was to have a daddy who was a doctor. But all I could think was that if you wanted Mary Janes, *wasn't it better to have a daddy who sold shoes?*

No Access, Whatsoever

I GREW UP VERY POOR in the countryside in Puerto Rico, and truly access was not there, whatsoever. I had two sisters—and then a brother who was born when I was eleven. So we were three girls, and my mother was a single mother.

Getting to the city to go food shopping or pay bills—became a journey for the day, the whole day. And finding a job was difficult, given where we lived. However, we lived in an area where everyone had similar limitations, so we didn't really know what we were missing. We never asked our mother why she didn't have any money. It was just part of growing up, and that was okay.

I had a child at seventeen and a half, and shortly after that we moved to the United States. Once I started college, I was still poor! But of course I had more access. College to me was a gift, and a door that opened at some point, and I just . . .

went on through. But it was never part of my expectations growing up.

> *Somewhere, on the edge of consciousness there is what I call a mythical norm, which each one of us within our hearts knows "that is not me." In America, this norm is usually defined as white, thin, male, young, heterosexual, Christian, and financially secure. It is with this mythical norm that the trappings of power reside.*
>
> —Audre Lorde

Class List

MAVERICK.
Plymouth Rock.
Upper middle.
Upper middle class.

Born to working class parents, upwardly mobile Jews in New York City. So I'm a worker, yeah, and solidly middle class.

Middle class. I'd say I've stepped up. Everybody in America is middle class.

Medium class. Not low class, not high class. Average.

I see a continuum from my grandparents to myself, sliding slowly down.

Currently—a class of elegance. Growing up: ah! A class of hard work and a school of hard knocks.

Do you want my class of origin, or my current class? Because I think there's a real difference.

GENDER STUDIES

I don't want your green-back dollar,
I don't want your diamond ring . . .

—American folksong

I T IS PAINFULLY COMMON for women to blame ourselves for our financial struggles, to feel that we alone are clumsy and incompetent. For almost all of us, such behavior goes back to earliest childhood, when our brothers were educated about money, and we, as daughters, weren't. Even now, many girls believe they "just can't manage money" as well as the men in the family, and "buy into" (an interesting term) that learned helplessness. "I grew up thinking that finance and money belonged to a secret society that only males were allowed into," writes psychotherapist Kate Levinson.[1]

Even though the top ten money-earning chores are the same for both sexes, boys are paid more for doing them than girls. At times, that bias extends to the allowance itself. "*Ooh, talk about gender and money!*" crowed a woman I interviewed, now an associate professor at Vermont Law School. "When I was in high school, I got five dollars a week, and I believe my brother got twenty, so he could afford to take girls out on dates." It was her job, she said, *to be asked out.*

Such inequities stretch their tentacles far into the future, as girls grow up into young women, and those women make their way into the working world. The average woman can expect to earn $430,480 less than the average white man over the course of her life, though the amount varies tremendously depending on her ethnic background.[2] Asian American women have the smallest lifetime pay deficit, while for Native American, black, and Latina women the amount is considerably more. "If working women earned the same salaries as working men with the same education and experience," writes Ariel Gore, "our family incomes would rise by $4,000 a year."[3]

↚

Frances: The Diamond Ring

WE STARTED TO TALK ABOUT DIVORCE just before Passover. I went to the vault to get out my engagement ring. And—it wasn't there! So I went home, and I said to Howard, "I can't imagine what happened—but my engagement ring is not in the vault." And he said, "No, I took it." And I remember thinking, Was it mine or was it his? It was just the most—upsetting—I can still feel it—as if I were somehow being struck in the stomach. I said, "What do you mean, you took it?" He said, "Well, I had it appraised, and I'm probably going to sell it, 'cause I'm going to need the money."

And I took all the rest of the jewelry he'd given me, including my wedding ring, and threw it at him, and said, *"I don't want any of this!"*

I was so upset, so enraged. I realized for the first time, very starkly, that it wasn't really mine. It was something he'd invested in, a symbol of the alliance. I'm not even saying marriage. And the alliance was over, so he would reclaim his property.

He actually said to me, "You never wear it." I said, "Where am I going to wear it? To Harlem, where I'm doing my research in single-room-occupancy hotels? To the grocery store?" "Well, if you don't wear it, what's the difference?"

It was a square-cut diamond of nearly four carats. It was beautiful. He had been in that business, and he knew how to get something good. I didn't care. At some level I didn't really care. What was upsetting was that something I had thought of as mine, wasn't mine. And I realized then that the house I lived in was his too, and that in a very real sense I was a nonperson. He was getting on with his life, and mine was over, in his eyes. It was brutal, very brutal. I got quite hysterical.

But since I don't really care about stuff, I got over it pretty quickly!

↫

In 2013, a study found that a woman earning more than her male partner could increase the risk of divorce by 50%, while one from 2015 claimed that earning less money made partners more likely to cheat."

Eva Wiseman

Suzanne: Playing Fair

THE BIGGEST STRUGGLE in my marriage has been about division of labor in the household. My husband and I both started out with academic jobs. But I decided to negotiate a half-time contract. Which turned out to be one of those things where you work full-time, but you only get half-time pay.

It was *not* a good arrangement.

So right off the bat, I'm making half the amount that Tim is making, plus he's in the sciences and I'm in the social sciences, so there's another disparity right there. He got promoted before I did, and so on. So we struggled and struggled and struggled. I was mad at him for ten years. Ten years! I was furious, because I did almost all the housework. All little-kid work. And I just couldn't figure out why he didn't help more!

Then at some point it became clear to me that *he was counting*, he had some rough notion of fairness. It's not that he was a jerk. I mean, I'm still married to him. I love him dearly. But he was calculating at some level, what was due. So he put in maybe ten or twenty percent of the work. Which was less, of course, than it should have been, but nonetheless.

I finally understood it when I left my job. I was without income for . . . I guess four years. And Tim stopped doing anything. *Anything at all.* It was as if he felt, "Okay, now *you* do the thing at home, 'cause that's what you want. And I'm really going to concentrate on my job, 'cause now *I'm* the total provider."

And then, just when I was about to despair, I had the most

curious thing happen. I went back to work, and very quickly I got promoted into an administrative position, and I started making *more* money than Tim was making. Which was a total shock. I'd never imagined I would close that gap. I'd resigned myself to thinking, *The most I can hope for is thirty percent. . . .*

But, by golly, when I started making more money than he did, *he* started pitching in—I mean, he now does *half the work in the house! At least!* We'd fought about this for years and years. So this time around it didn't even cross my mind to say, "Why don't you do more?" The kids were older, I knew that I could handle it. I wasn't expecting anything from him. And then, all of a sudden, the thing shifted, and that's where it's been ever since.

I remember I said to a friend, "At some level, I just know that he's been *calculating* this." But it was a big surprise to me, and I still don't know how I feel about it, honestly. There is a part of me that thinks, *Wait a minute! How do you put a figure on . . . ?"* I mean, I don't even know where to start! My career would have been totally different if Tim had done more. But on the other hand, it was reassuring to realize that some notion of fairness was involved.

But every once in a while he'll come up with some revisionist comment: how he feels really good that he stood by me all those years while I was working for my career. And I'm thinking, *What?! I did that* in spite of *all the other stuff at home!*

So now—I can't tell you how deliciously satisfying it feels to be making more money. I'm just *delighted!* We were just at the bank—we were taking out a second mortgage, to pay for our child's private school—and the loan officer asked us, "Who wants to be the primary person on this loan?" And we kind of looked at each other, and she said, "Well, who's making more money?" And Tim turned to me and said, "I think it's you at this point." And then we had to get our pay stubs, and figure out exactly how much we were making, which we don't usually do. And right now I'm making a hundred and seven thousand, and he's making ninety-three.

The college pays its administrators ridiculously well, so I feel a little funny to be making this kind of money. But I'm totally happy—you know—to have evened this out between us.

❧

Gender & Money

OOH, TALK ABOUT GENDER and money! When I was in high school, I got five dollars a week, and I believe my brother got twenty, so he could afford to take girls out on dates. It was my job *to be asked out*.

And I got paid to study, also. I got paid! A dollar for every A, fifty cents for every A minus, and twenty dollars, plus an R-rated film, for all As!

❧

The Two Purses

MY FATHER WAS THE BREADWINNER, and my mother stayed at home. The only cash she had was her "allowance."

She kept the household money in a purse that she called "Peter," and the clothes money in another purse called "Paul." She'd tuck a scrap of paper in each one, and keep a running tally. Often, at the end of the month, if our clothes had cost more than she had budgeted for, she'd rob Peter to pay Paul (or vice versa).

She hated having to ask for anything more.

↤

Women are men without money.

—Paul Samuelson

The 99¢ Special

OH MY GOSH, do I have stories! So, growing up working class, my dad worked two, sometimes three jobs. He was a letter carrier, he taught Hebrew School. And occasionally he would deliver pizza. And then when I was in first grade, my mom went back and worked for the government part-time.

And money was—*I feel it!*—I can feel the distress, even today. Like when I go to pay bills. My mom was in charge of the bills, and she *could not wrap her head around money.* For instance, if she owed you twenty dollars, and you owed her ten, she'd have to give you the twenty dollars, and you'd have to give her the ten. I remember thinking that was, like, so backward.

Occasionally, we'd go out to breakfast at the diner, and with my mom we always had to get the 99¢ special. But when we went with my dad, we could have anything we wanted. Somehow he always seemed to have extra, even though he was completely turning over his paycheck. Either he skimmed some off the top, or he kept his tips.

But it was so clear with my mom: everything we got was on sale. Like if we'd go to the store and there was a pair of jeans. "Oh," she'd say. "I'll get these for your birthday!" But then I wouldn't want them. 'Cause I would want to be surprised. I remember in middle school, having two pairs of jeans I wore every day, alternating, and always thinking that my friends had so much more.

⁎

Scarlett O'Hara

MY FATHER ALWAYS HAD A SHORT TEMPER. He went from being a wild teenager—very smart, very immature—straight into college, and then on to medical school. He was a doctor and he was in private practice, and as far as he was concerned, everyone he dealt with was beneath him: his wife who was always very accommodating—his two children, and the people who worked in his office. So he became a dictator: like command and control. And my mother didn't stand up for herself.

And when I was a teenager, I began to notice this. I remember one time—it was as petty as how come she didn't cook the steak the way he liked it, or his shirts weren't pressed the way he wanted them. And I said, "Well, if you don't like it, *why don't you do it yourself?*" And that did not go over very well.

My mother and I went for a walk together, after the blow-up, and I asked her point-blank, "Why don't you leave him, if he treats you like this?" And she said, *"I can't. I have no money."* And that was a *very* defining moment for me. I told myself, like Scarlett O'Hara, "That *will* not happen to me. I will *never* be in that situation." I understood that I needed to be independent of my father, and independent of anyone, any man, financially.

And that really did inform a lot of my career choices.

The greatest gift every girl can have is economic independence.
—Helen Mirren

1."I grew up thinking . . .": Kate Levinson, *Emotional Currency: A Woman's Guide to Building a Healthy Relationship with Money* (Berkeley, CA, Celestial Arts, 2011).
2."The average woman can expect to earn . . .": See "Gender Pay Gap in the United States" on Wikipedia, quoting from an analysis of Census Bureau data released by Reach Advisors in 2008
3."If working women earned the same salaries as working men . . .": Ariel Gore, *Bluebird: Women and the New Psychology of Happiness* (New York, Farrar, Straus & Giroux, 2010).

NOT MAKING IT

*We dealt with hunger. We dealt with cold. We were the
ones who held things together. Knit one, purl one. We
were the ones who, after working all day, made the meals.
. . . We were the ones who, if the cupboard was bare, faced
the open mouths of our children. . . . We knew the limits. .
. . We knew the length of caring.*

—Susan Griffin

"WE SPEND MOST OF THE HOURS and the days of our
lives hearing, explaining, complaining, or worrying
about what we don't have enough of," writes Lynne Twist.[4]
"Of course we don't have enough money—ever. . . . Before
we even sit up in bed, before our feet touch the floor, we're
already inadequate, already behind, already losing, already
lacking something." In the section that follows, you can
practically feel that terror seething off the page.

*I began to feel like a financial oncologist.
Oh my God! Like an epidemic had hit.*

For those at the lower end of the social scale, such terror has a thorough grounding in reality. Consider Tashi, a Tibetan refugee from India, who moved to the United States in her early twenties. From her first pitiful earnings, she managed to send $3,000 back to her family in Mysore. "I never spend anything," she told me. "I just *save-save-save-save* and I send it all back home."

But that sense of panicked insufficiency shows up in a surprising number of women's money stories, however comfortably ensconced they might appear to be. More than a quarter of women with household incomes over $200,000 still entertain serious fears about becoming a bag lady.[5] On one hand, such fears are highly unrealistic. But there is a certain aching accuracy to them too. Because women live on average five to seven years longer than men, most of us will outlive our spouses.[6] And those years can be difficult ones, both practically and financially. Some 9 percent of elderly women in the United States now live at or below the federal poverty line, meaning that, for far too many of us, the imagined bag lady is only a step or two away.[7]

↫

Where's the Money Going to Come From?

I began to feel like a financial oncologist.

Oh my God! Like an epidemic had hit.

Competent? Not really.

Sometimes I can't bear to open my bank statements.

Rent is my biggest issue.

We pay $750 a month, but nothing is included.

I used to get food stamps and cash assistance.
But now the clock is ticking
and I have to find a job.

During the job interview,
they asked how much I'd want to make.

And I just threw a number out there.
I said thirty thousand.

But I don't really know how much money you spend in a year.
Like how much it takes to actually survive.

Mummy and Daddy were no help at all.
And I've never been practical.

And really, I'm everything I'd say a feminist shouldn't be,
which is to say I married Ari

and he's really good with numbers,
and I mostly say, "Okay, fine, you figure it out!"

I've sat with clients,
where I hand them a statement,
and you can see their eyes just glaze over.

They can't see the relationship:
why this number is bigger than this,

or how you calculate a yield.
They can't even absorb it.

And what I remember thinking was,

How could these very bright women be so stupid about money?

⟵

Not Making It

I HAVE VERY SUCCESSFULLY AVOIDED making money. And I have wanted more.

I have felt the envy and the sorry-for-myself that I can't *da-da-da....*

At the same time, when the choices come up, "Will this make you more money, or will that?" I always go for the one that will make less.

⟵

Tashi: I Don't Spend Anything

I DON'T HAVE ANY INCOME. I don't think there is anyone, so far, make less than me.

My full name Tashi Pema Dorje. I was born in Mysore, India, in 1976. My parents are from Tibet, but they got refugee in India, and my mom's a housewife—do nothing, just take care of children. And then my dad—he worked in Tibetan political government, more like serving his country—to help others.

And then he do a little kind of a business, like buy things from India, then go to Tibet, and sell. But he didn't make any money in whole his life, so I didn't really see him in that way.

What did I learn about money growing up? I don't know how to answer that.

When I was in the Tibetan village school, I have pocket money from my long vacation. All of my relatives they give money and I pile it up. But then it's over, and I want—I want money so that I can wear nice clothes, so I can, like, catch up to my other friends. And also to eat snacks when I am hungry.

And I don't have those, much.

When I was twenty-one, I went to Europe. I got a visa to Denmark, and I worked in a Tibetan restaurant. I wasn't supposed to work there because I'm a tourist, but then I did. I made momo and stuff like that. They pay me cash.

The pay was around, like, forty kroner. Yeah, forty kroner per hour.

When I go back to India, I have some money saved. I gave my dad money to buy a bike for him, a Honda. It was the first time I made money, and I gave him something really he should have. It gave me pleasure.

↵

At least 43 million immigrants, documented and undocumented, reside in the United States.

—Jose Antonio Vargas

I used to get food stamps, and I used to get cash assistance. And now the clock is ticking, and I have to find a job. I'm trying to become an LPN [licensed practical nurse] and if I can, I don't know.

My husband, me, and my three children, we have five in the family. Rent is not big because it's housing-subsidized. Food we can make. And welfare is good, they give a lot of food stamps.

But then I have to have the phone, and Internet, and stuff like that. And so it's really tight.

But you know, I don't spend much. Like when I first came here in United States—I cannot even spend one dollar. Because I always count like Indian rupees for that, and I have to send it back. My friends, sometimes they treat me, that's a different thing. But I never spend anything. I just *save-save-save-save*, and I send it all back home.

I send maybe three thousand back to India. Three thousand in one year. It's because I never spend, even a dollar. There's some guys here, they are really hardworking, they work, work. But they always run out of money, because they spend on cigarettes. They don't save. For me, it's a little different. I have a little money in my hand, to be on safe side, but I haven't spend them.

I've been like whole of my life short of money. It's just—my nature.

Being a mom, I have my little ones to take care of. I have to have a nice house for them to be raised in. The men are also thinking that way, but they don't have that motherly attach with the children. My husband—he's not a spending kind of guy. When I wanted to buy something for my children, he would say, "That's not necessary!" But I'm spending for my children, I'm not spending for myself!

I never spend for myself, even like fast food, hot dogs, not even I was hungry. I don't do that.

If I should really have to treat myself—just a cute little

ring, maybe. Buy a beautiful ring? But that's not really necessary. I don't know! It's like I torture myself, to save money for others.

I'm very responsible, yes.

My deepest wish? I wish to have a lot of money, make a lot of money, so that I can provide the comfort life for my children. And "go green" maybe. Because I'm worried not only about money, I'm worried about ending the world. Because if we don't have a natural resource, how can we even survive? There will be no life.

We did not have much income. We had love and work and play instead.

—Mary Oliver

Rosa: The Family Pot

I WAS BORN IN PORTUGAL IN 1953, and I don't remember money. I don't remember wanting anything except—the grapes that were grown there, or the figs.

Everyone I knew was growing their own food. They raised their own meat, and they made cloth. One grandmother made linen. We planted the flax, and we had wool from her sheep. We had milk—goats' milk—and we made cheese.

They bought coffee and sugar and rice. And cotton cloth: things like that. Bananas were a rare luxury. 'Cause the climate didn't work for that. I always knew that there was plenty, but it was gotten by constant labor, constant year-round labor.

You know, in Portugal, it was very clear: you were poor or you were rich. There's only recently a middle class in Portugal. Back then, there wasn't. And as a child, you kind of go, "Why?"

You don't get it.

You'd hear people say, "*E rica,*" she's rich. And then they would be like, "*E muito pobre.*" She's very poor. And usually it was *she* was very poor, not *he* was very poor. And she was poor because there wasn't a man to help. Or the man was always drinking and she was too sick to grow her own food. So we would bring her food.

And those things stay with you.

After we moved to the States, we all lived in the kitchen. And that wasn't true in other homes. They had, like, the den and the family room and the formal living room and the formal dining room and the kitchen with the breakfast nook, and everybody had their separate bedroom. And you didn't have to walk through one room to get to another the way you did in our house.

For a long time I didn't know that we were poor. But even then, it was very confusing, because, "Okay, so we don't have these things, but we're not like *those* people who are poor!"

I remember some neighbors whose home was almost barren. There was rarely food there. It was very dirty. They were really down-and-out. And it was shocking as a child to see that. Our house wasn't always clean, and nothing matched. It wasn't like

House Beautiful. But there was a certain homeyness I didn't see in that place.

⤺

My dad worked really hard in the leather tanneries. And then somehow, we all went to Portugal for three months every summer. I don't know how he did that. I truly don't.

I have almost no money. But there's this poverty mentality I don't think I've ever had.

We had a "family pot," and all the money went into that pot. For example, I bought a brand-new car when I was very young and I paid cash for it. When I was nineteen? Maybe eighteen, actually. But by then I had been working for years and years. So when I needed a car, the money was there to pay for it. I had earned it. But it came out of the family pot.

When I got married, my parents, who were of very small means, gave me ten thousand dollars to put down on a house. *How the hell did they get that money?* I mean, that was cash! And at a time when nine thousand dollars was a yearly salary if you were lucky. So that was pretty remarkable.

But it doesn't feel like generosity. It just feels like that's the way this family is.

⤺

My first husband never made a lot of money. He wasn't able to go to school and get a degree, so the jobs he got were never very lucrative. I helped him start a business before I left. In a way I was taking care of myself too, 'cause that gave him the money to pay child support.

My second husband had a good education, and a good job. But he's really bad with money. And he and I got into lots of trouble because of that.

And my brother is a nitwit about money. Always lived beyond his means, big-time! He was very acquisitive, very extravagant, and he lost his business, lost his house—went bankrupt. His house was repossessed.

Out in the world, what I mostly see is that men have more access to money. Women get left carrying the burden. Just because they bear the children and are responsible for them— they get slowed down. But it's a very true fact that women make less money than men. Women can be doing the same job and getting less. And that's still true even today.

⟵

I had to declare bankruptcy this year. I forget the exact figure, but it might have been a hundred and thirty thousand. *A lot of money!* And most of that was big debt.

But I'm very aware of the other debts, the smaller ones. For instance, I owe eight hundred dollars to my dentist and eight hundred dollars to my doctor. And I have other debts too, like the guy who just came and cleaned the furnace ducts. There's maybe a thousand dollars' worth of bills I owe. . . .

But I own the house outright, and that's an asset, they can't take it away from me. And I'm making little bits of money selling stuff. Once those little debts are paid, and the big debt has gone away, I think I should be okay.

But the bankruptcy affects my credit, which has always

been excellent. I used those credit cards when my sister was in trouble and we didn't have a way to pay the lawyer. And when my dad died and didn't leave any money, and we had to bury him.

You have the credit and that's when you use it. It can be a trap.

I have gotten to a place where I am better at earmarking money, "Okay, this has to go here. And this has to go here." 'Cause it's easy to spend five and ten and fifteen dollars and then not have enough for some bill.

My daughters always say, "You just need envelopes!" How did they get to be so sensible? Cause we never had money the whole time they were growing up.

I can be very extravagant in the garden. Paying twenty-two dollars for a rose is very significant for someone like me. But I kept dreaming about this one rose. Three nights out of the week, I dreamt there was this New Dawn rose, and the third time, I said, "I'm just going to go buy that damn rose."

And I went and did that.

Plus I'll always put food back in order to get Dr. Hauschka face cream and cleanser. Because that stuff is nourishing in a way that's unbelievable. When my kids were little, I wouldn't put back the milk, but I would put back coffee. I wouldn't get the coffee. But I'd get Dr. Hauschka!

Upstairs in my little meditation space I put up this sign that says—what does it say? *"Create your own prosperity."*

Often, when I'm working, I'll find money on the floor. Not a lot of money, but like a quarter, a dime, pennies.

And I pick it up and I put it in my shoe.

And I do this weird little meditation. It's like "Okay, a dollar or ten dollars or a hundred dollars, maybe even a thousand dollars is going to come my way."

Because the truth is, you never know.

Dysfunctional

MY SISTERS AND I ALL FEEL the same way, that somehow we're failures in the money realm. We somehow feel . . . incompetent, or stupid, I don't exactly know what it is. There's some hidden source of anxiety that I haven't to this day quite put my finger on. But the failure is beyond any kind of reasonable, right-sized way of thinking about the problem. And since my husband is equally dysfunctional, it's an area that we both stay away from. So things pile up, and it's like a negative cycle.

I just wish that I were willing to *interact* with it. Like *deal with it.* You know, I'm terrible. Everything in my life comes and goes; it's all automatic payment. I don't ever look at my paychecks. I just don't. And I feel on some level like I *should.* Like it would give me *satisfaction* to be more in touch with it, and to be better—to just have more ownership of it all.

Immigrant Mentality

BOTH MY PARENTS WERE IMMIGRANTS, so I've been accused of having an "immigrant mentality" toward money.

Like, "What can you get? How can you work this? There's four pieces of paper here, how can I divide it and make eight?" I don't think I've ever bought anything that wasn't on sale. Why should you? Why should you pay fifty percent over the real price? Why? What's the point?

But I learned all those adult lessons the really hard way. The first time I got nailed with capital gains taxes, I wanted to cut off my legs, I was so upset. Nobody ever told me. Nobody ever taught me about hair products, stocks, bonds, how to take care of your clothes, how to cook. 'Cause my mother—may she rest in peace—she had her hands full, just living.

↬

"Fourteenth of March, I think it was," he said.
"Fifteenth," said the March Hare.
"Sixteenth," added the Dormouse.
"Write all that down," the King said to the jury, and the jury eagerly wrote down all three dates on their slates, and then added them up, and reduced the answer to shillings and pence.

—Lewis Carroll

Husbands & Wives

WHEN I FIRST MET ROB, he had a checkbook; it would just say, "Joan," and I'd say, "Well, who's Joan?" And he'd say, "I don't know." The checkbook was thousands of dollars in the red, he'd no idea. And at that moment my fate was sealed. 'Cause if I'd met a guy who was good with money, I would have ceded over that part of my life, happily! But I met a guy who was not good with money. So I became the good-with-money person. I hate it! But he hates it more. So that became my role.

§

Money Management

I BECAME A MOTHER AT SEVENTEEN. And I didn't start working until I was in college. So, to me, money management was very difficult. To me, money management was: you get paid, you pay the bills, and—there's nothing left.

I had been in a relationship where I had to do that, and I hated it. I would leave it to the last minute, I would bounce checks here and there because "I thought I paid that bill!" "No, that bill is double," or I wouldn't manage it so well. I would struggle with it. So when Randi came into my life, it was clear to us that, "She's good at it, go for it!" I have complete trust, and I love it. I totally love it.

Before she came, it was my salary alone, paying for all these bills, so there was no way that I could have done all that we do now, now the salary's suddenly doubled. She introduced me to this new style of life. When you look at it, it's like, "Oh, perfect! Now we have enough to pay the bills, and enough to travel, enough to save, and just be comfortable!"

§

Go Figure

All those terms we half understand . . .

Inflation, deflation, consumer confidence
Bearish, bullish, free market enterprise
Billions, trillions . . .

Subprime mortgages.

How many zeroes is that, again?

Hedge funds, arbitrage, collateral, derivatives.
Bailouts, buyouts, compound interest*

Junk bonds, bottom line, Ponzi schemes, mortgage-backed
securities, predatory lending

What does it mean?

Could you just explain?

I should never have trusted him.

I should never . . .

Short-selling, call options, quantitative easing
Balance sheets, hung out to dry, oh my God, foreclosures!

Liabilities, depreciation

I just don't understand!

Gilt-edged securities, hostile takeovers
Diversify, liquidify, commodity futures . . .
Freeze the salaries, slash the budgets, cancel or defer . . .

---

*According to a 2008 survey, two-thirds of Americans do not
understand how compound interest works.

In the fall of 2009, Elinor Ostrom received the Nobel Prize for Economics—the first woman ever to be honored in this way. Her research had to do with extra-market economic transactions.

I wouldn't worry your pretty little head about all that . . .

---

4. "We spend most of the hours and the days of our lives hearing, explaining, complaining . . .": Lynne Twist, *The Soul of Money: Transforming Your Relationship with Money and Life* (New York, W. W. Norton, 2003).

5. "Twenty-seven percent of women with household incomes over $200,000 still entertain serious fears about becoming a bag lady." Amy Langfield speaking on *NBC News* on Monday, April 1, 2013, quoting an online survey by Allianz Life Insurance Company of North America.

6. "Women live on average five to seven years longer than men." Life expectancy for women in the United States is 81.32 years, cf. 76.4 years for men. Shervin Assari, "The Conversation," on World Economic Forum, March 14, 2017.

7. "Some 9 percent of U.S women age sixty-five and older . . . live at or below the federal poverty level, which is just $11,880 for individuals, and $16,020 for a family of two." Elizabeth O'Brien, "Older Women 80 Percent More Likely Than Men to Be Impoverished." Market Watch, March 2, 2017.

COUNTING IT OUT

The king was in the countinghouse
counting out his money.
The queen was in the parlor,
eating bread and honey.

—Nursery rhyme

S O GOES THE OLD FAMILIAR NURSERY RHYME. But
what if the queen is the one in the countinghouse, not
the king? *What happens then?* This section opens with the
story of Aurora, who now works professionally as a financial
advisor. Unlike most girls, she was taught to manage money
as a child. Her parents gave her an allowance every quarter. And from the time she was ten, they also required her to
submit a budget.

More than half a lifetime later, Aurora remains practical
and clearheaded about money, utterly competent and capable.
Others may not be so lucky—or so skilled. But even for them,
the act of handling money—keeping track—can become a
source of satisfaction and relief. I think of the waitress who re-
turns from work and throws all her change into a big container, then counts it painstakingly into tall glass jars, or the young
mother who hides coins under the sofa cushions or behind the

clock, and encourages her kids to go on a money hunt. That way, she explains, "You never feel like you are broke."

Dollars & Sense

Money is the source of my deepest anxieties.
I always felt I was on the brink of catastrophe.

It was really painful trial and error and bumping into things,
and, you know, figuring them out over time.

Money was a major point of contention
between my husband and me.

He'd pay the bills by not paying the rent.
We were evicted from many lovely houses.

After I divorced, I had years of panic.
And fantasies of being a bag lady, and

"I can't possibly make enough to live on."
But I did! I always did. I had enough. And I think I still do.

Aurora: Chief Financial Officer

I ALWAYS GOT AN ALLOWANCE, and at some point there was a chore that went along with that. It was just expected.

And then, when I was around ten, my parents told me I'd

have to submit a budget. There were different line items, and I had to project how much I was going to need. If I wanted to go to the movies, I had to put that in. If I wanted to buy a forty-five, that was my responsibility. They were very clear about how you figure things out. If a movie costs fifty cents, and you think you're going to go twice a month, then that's a dollar a month times twelve months of the year, so you put twelve dollars in your budget.

It started in the fall, because the fiscal year corresponded with the school year. But there were a lot more expenses in the first three months, because of school supplies and Christmas and two family birthdays. So I had to figure out what my lump sum was, and rough out what I was going to need, and then I told them, "Okay, from September through December 31, I'm going to need four dollars and thirty-seven cents a week, and from January 1 to August 31, I'll only need three dollars a week," or whatever it was.

But my budgets were always approved, and I always had money when I needed it.

And I was taught about savings very young. I was an extra in a movie—it was called *Lilith*, starring Jean Seberg and Warren Beatty. I was in third grade, maybe eight years old, and I got paid twenty-five dollars a day! So my parents said, "You're opening a bank account," and that money got deposited.

And from then, I always had a savings account with something in it.

I must have been okay in math, because my father would have me help him every tax time. He'd have all these slips of paper and receipts on the table, and he'd ask me to total them all up. I'd sit there with an adding machine, and that was my job.

I have a definitive memory from that time, that it's just how you conduct yourself—*you don't spend unnecessarily.* That there's something sort of sinful about waste, about acquisitiveness. . . .

In terms of clothing, my mom got real smart with me. She announced, "Okay, I'm going to spend two hundred dollars on your clothing. You decide what items you want, and I will subtract that from this two hundred." And it was so smart! Because every time we'd go to the store, and I'd go, *"Oh, wow! Look at that! I want it, I want it!"* she'd say, "Okay, I'll subtract that from your account."

And I would pause. "Well, I don't know. There might be something later I want more. I don't know."

She taught me about mix-and-match, how if you got this plain black skirt, then you could put this top and this top and this top and this top with it, and have six outfits with one skirt. . . .

Even when I was given something extra, a legitimate financial argument was made for it. For example, I decided to go to Europe as soon as I graduated from high school. I saved my babysitting money, and I taught swimming in the summers, and I saved that money too, because *I was going to do this. I was going to do this!* My mother wanted to give me a little bit of a boost. But what she said was, "I figured out what it costs to feed you, and since you'll be gone for sixty days, here's the amount I would have been spending on your food."

> *If you're bourgeois, money is it. It's all the questions and all the answers. Ain't no E-flat or color blue, only $12.98 or $1,000. If it isn't money, it isn't nothing.*
>
> —John Coltrane

I've been married three times, and my financial experience with each husband has been different. But I've always been the primary money person. My husband now refers to me as "the Chief Financial Officer."

I've never, ever understood separate money, when you're married. Lots of people do that. You know, "my money, his money." It makes no sense to me. "What are you talking about? You're a unit! You're a team, you're working toward common goals." So we have a loose rule that if we're going to spend more than a hundred bucks or so, we discuss it with each other.

I will admit that when I knew I needed to get out of my first marriage, I started keeping a secret savings account, so I'd be sure to have the money to leave. And since I was managing the money, *he didn't notice!*

I had this one girlfriend who wanted to get out of her marriage. I told her, "You have to start saving on your own." She

says, "He goes through everything of mine. He'll find out."
I said, "Then you're going to use my address, I'll keep your
books here." But she said she needed to have her deposit slip
so she could make deposits, the one with her name printed
on it, "and how am I going to hide that from my husband?"

Well . . .

We took a tampon applicator, pulled the tampon out of it,
and left the cardboard. Then, very carefully, I took an X-acto
knife and split the wrapper open on the outside, rolled up the
deposit slip, stuck it in where the tampon used to be, and put
it back inside the paper wrapper, so it would look like just a
tampon in her purse.

I don't know how I came up with that, but it worked! She
was able to save the money, and she got out of an abusive
relationship.

❦

I've always been able to do the things I want to do. And I've
always lived within my means. I tell my friends, "Debt is
personal sabotage. You want to change your life, get yourself out of debt." I *withhold* doing certain things, *so* that I can
spend on that.

I didn't understand why other people didn't live like me,
at first. I remember thinking, *How could these very bright wom-
en be so stupid about money?*

❦

And then when I was in my late forties, I decided to take a
trip. I had to travel. I just had to! I was working at the Uni-

versity of Massachusetts at the time, and everybody kept saying, "How can you do that? How can you do that?" *I can do that because I didn't buy a Starbucks coffee every day. I packed my lunch instead of buying it. I didn't go crazy buying Christmas presents. I chose to save.* And I traveled for *eight months!*

I'd been dreaming about this trip for a long time, and I kept thinking I should wait until I found a travel buddy. A partner, a honey. For so long I'd been going, "Oh, woe is me, no husband, no children, no house!" And then one day I woke up, and I said, "Wait a minute! No husband, no children, no house! *I am outta here!*"

↤

Indeed, I thought, slipping the silver into my purse, it is remarkable . . . what a change of temper a fixed income will bring about. . . . Food, house, and clothing are mine forever.

—Virginia Woolf

Michelle: A Warm Fuzzy

MY NAME IS MICHELLE, and I am fifty-eight years old. I was a college professor for the last ten years, and I just lost that job. So I'm looking for a new career right now.

But I'm an artist, so I can fit in any society. I can be with kings and queens. I have good manners. *Classy!* My mother was Slovak; she had Czechish airs. It was very important to her to give me "brains, beauty, and breeding." Those were her "three b's."

I was always a saver. If my allowance was fifty cents, by the end of the year I'd have twenty dollars. I've always understood the need to have what I call "a warm fuzzy." A little stash.

My father "paved paradise and put up a parking lot." And when he died, there were seven vultures at the door, with their shoulders up around here, 'cause my father's estate was valued at two million with debits at six million. He was a real estate agent—and he was a huckster. He was a grocery clerk who made good deals and he was a visionary—who bought me my house twenty years after he died. And who gave me my warm fuzzy. "Thank you, Daddy!"

And after that, my mother went to work. My little immigrant concentration-camp-survivor mother went into his office to try and stave away the vultures. And she did a good job, God bless her. May she rest in peace! She bought from my father's estate these two little buildings—my husband said, "They're just strip malls with a fancy front"—a little strip mall, in Akron, Ohio. *But they bought me my freedom!*

↩

My feeling about money has always been, "It's a good thing to have a little, and don't want what you can't afford." And now I'm married to a man whose values are *the antithesis* of that. And it's hard. Because I never felt poor, never felt like I didn't have, never felt I wasn't capable to consort with kings and queens and gods and goddesses. My own sense was, "I have plenty!" And now I say, "Well, maybe I *should* want." And I don't want to want what I can't afford. I *like* not wanting. I *like* being satisfied. I like having enough to have that "fuck-you money"—you know, if I don't want to be here, I can leave.

I can live really simply. I can live like a rat. Not like a rat. *Simply!*

Errgh! Well, my husband just went bankrupt. And he went bankrupt in the best way. He waited until all of his obligations to his ex-wife and his children were met, so that nobody would come after *them*. And then *he* went bankrupt. And we've been in therapy about this, and I've come to see that he just doesn't care. And he *wants!* "This is beyond its usable life," that's his tone. "Why's it beyond its usable life? Fix it! Call the repairman." "Naw, it's beyond its useable life." And that's really tough for me. We have a joint account, which he floats and I float, and from time to time we look like we are solvent.

But no, I will not, absolutely not merge our bank accounts, 'cause he has no relationship to money. I mean, his own mother says, "Don't give him a credit card."

↤

One time, I got ripped off for fifty-five thousand dollars. Some son-of-a-bitch, his name was Marvin Waldman, and please use it. Because he's still around ripping people off. I ran into him eighteen years later. He's a shyster. He's, like, a white-collar criminal, and he had a deal. His story was, "There's this man and his daughter, they're building houses in Saranac Lake, and if you give me an investment now, I'll triple it in three years." I thought, *Great, I'll give him fifty-five thousand dollars, I'll have a hundred and fifty thousand. Cool!* So I gave him fifty-five thousand dollars—and his check bounced.

I had met the woman who turned me on to him at an ashram, and the moral of this story is, "Never take your checkbook to an ashram." *Euagh!* He ripped me off for fifty-five grand. It's a lot of money, even now.

I sued him, but he went bankrupt. That was awful! I ran into him years later at one of the big Hudson Valley estates. And so we're there, and he's there, and we're standing at this staircase, and he says, "Don't I know you?" and I think, *I've fucked a lot of men in my life*: "Maybe, what's your name?" "Marvin Waldman." I felt like, you know, *there's the devil.* There he is. I am looking at the devil. And I just said, *"You know me."* And I turned on my heels and went inside. And ran right into my friend Ricky, which was perfect, because I could tell him the whole story. I mean, to tell anyone you've been hornswoggled out of fifty-five thousand dollars is not something you want to admit to in your life.

It's made me a very cautious investor. I never take chances, *ever, ever, ever.* That's the lesson I learned from that one. I said to him, "You are in my backyard, and I am telling all these people exactly who you are. Just so you know." And he left that night.

But I've always thought I was really lucky. My parents gave me good values, a good education, a good head on my shoulders, and they left me a warm fuzzy. It wasn't massive, it was never massive. But I always walked around feeling like *I had all the money in the world.* "You don't have any money? I'll take you out!" Because I've always felt and believed that that was correct. The correct behavior. That I had abundance.

My little legacy that I inherited thirty years ago, that went up, down, whatever, I always felt like it was millions, until I started to realize, "Oh, there are things you're supposed to want." And then I thought, *No, you're not!* Let's get real here. I *do* live in abundance. I *do* have anything anyone could possibly want. Excuse me, but that's where I'm sitting here today.

↵

Counting It Out

I LOVE COUNTING MONEY! *I love it.* If you're in the casino you don't play with real money, but then you keep thinking about what it means. You look at that anonymous stack of chips and know that that's a thousand dollars, and so I love that.

Rob went up to deliver a table. And the guy owed him thirty-two hundred dollars, thirty-two hundred and fifty dollars. I wrote it down three times, because Rob is a little dyslexic and this guy was a little bit of an asshole. And Rob comes back, and he has a weird look on his face, and I say, "What happened?" and he goes, "I don't know." I say, "What does that mean?" He goes, "I counted the money three times, it keeps coming out different." So he hands me this stack of money, and there's a hundred dollar bill on the top, and I'm thinking to myself, *Awright* . . . and then I take out the bottom bill, and it's a twenty-dollar bill, and then I flip through it, there's fives. So I say, "Who gave you this?" And he says, "The guy." So I say, "Who counted it?" He says, "Me and the guy." So I say, "How did you count it? Show me." So he goes, "A hundred, a hundred and twenty, plus fifty is a hundred and seventy." I said, "Robbie, you put the hundreds together, you put the fifties."

So I counted it, and it was short, like, eighty dollars. I counted it again to be sure. I had Rob count it. I called the guy, and said, "Listen, Rob gave me this wad of money. It's short eighty dollars." He said, "It can't be. I counted it." I said, "Well, I counted it." He said, "Well, I'm a money guy." I started laughing. I said, "No, you're not!" He said, "What do you mean?" I said, "You had it all mixed up. You don't do that. You put the hundreds with the hundreds, the fifties with the fifties. This is—!!" He starts laughing, and he said, "I'll be in later. I'll give you the eighty bucks."

⤺

Rolling the Change

I TEND TO PAY IN CASH. And I usually don't give exact change, so I'm always getting change back in my purse. And then—this is funny to talk about—I put it all into a big container that I have. I just *put all the change in, put all the change in, put all the change in!* 'Cause I like to have access to it. So what I do when I start *panicking* about money, is I dump it out, and separate it. I have jars of, like, my quarters, my dimes, my nickels, and my pennies, all the way down.

And then, a lot of times, I'll feel better. I won't need to do anything else. I'll just leave it sorted. And then I'll build it up, and sort again, when I feel I need to.

But when I'm really panicky, I'll sit down and roll my change. I refuse to go to a Coinstar or anything like that. Because I want to spend the time rolling it. And I usually make intricate designs. So that's one of my little rituals. You know, I've paid my taxes through change I've rolled by hand!

I also tend to save my dollar bills. I bartend and wait tables, so I often have a surplus of dollar bills. I like to save those, because they always feel like a lot. It's like, *whoaaa!!* Then you count it, and you're like, "Huh! Seventy-five dollars!" On the other hand, you never know how much it's going to be. Plus it takes a lot of time to count out all the ones, versus, you know, twenty, forty, sixty. . . . And the time it takes to count it, makes me feel like it is more.

She has counted on this life continuing. She has counted on continuing. Every day she has counted, every day she has done what she must, done what she must to go on.
—Susan Griffin

We Started Talking

THIS WINTER IT WAS A LOT SLOWER at the restaurant. We weren't making the money we had been making and, I mean, I was feeling it! But I have a guaranteed income—the restaurant income is, like, extra! And for my coworkers, it's their only job. So we started talking, and I was like, "Tell me—tell me about your debt." And I gave all these assignments to this coworker of mine. "How much interest are you paying on your credit cards? Do you know how much you're paying? Write it down, I'll help you think this through. Like, bring it in." I'm like, "Go to the credit union. And consolidate some of this. It doesn't have to be this hard."

So that felt really good. When she actually went home and looked at her bills, and saw how much she was paying in interest—she was livid! I was like: *"You're getting hosed!"* I'm like: "Cancel this—move this! First of all, call these companies and tell them you don't want to pay that interest anymore. The worst they can do is say no. But move, move that shit— they're counting on people not paying attention. Like, yeah!"

Cabin Fever

I ALWAYS HIDE MONEY! I leave a little here, a little there— like singles and five-dollar bills. I have twenty dollars in the car, so if I need gas, I always feel like I have money. It's not a huge amount, but at any one time, it could be close to a hundred bucks.

I used to say to the kids, when they had cabin fever in the winter, "Okay, go on a money hunt!" And they'd look in my pockets, they'd search all over the house—and we'd have enough for maybe a pizza, maybe just an ice cream. But it was always fun. Like, "I wonder what we'll find!" And sometimes we found a *lot* of money, and we went for pizza *and* a movie. And invited another kid!

So you never feel like you're broke.

TAKING IT

Lack of money is the root of all evil.

—George Bernard Shaw

AGAIN AND AGAIN, LISTENING TO WOMEN TALK, I'd be reminded of the title of Adrienne Rich's book of essays, *On Lies, Secrets, and Silence*, now dating back almost a half century.[8] Talk about money is full of lies, secrets, and silence. Some of us have so much more—some so much less—and it can be painful and difficult to acknowledge the rifts. Some women steal, forge checks, or embezzle money; others describe how it feels to be deceived or stolen from. "I had a client who was going through a divorce," says psychic Clary Sage, "and she had no idea what her husband was worth. Never would look in the drawer. And she finds out he owns an airline, a department store, a vitamin company, and he's crying poverty! Oh, that really helped her. *Secrets, secrets, secrets!*"

Bryony: Treasure

I FOUND A BAG OF MONEY ONCE: real treasure! I was working at this little ma-and-pa shop in New Haven [Connecticut]. They were selling on the store to someone else, and they hired my friends and me to clear it out. We were supposed to clean it out, and trash everything that was left over, and then we had to paint and do repairs.

I was in the back corner of some closet and I was taking things and throwing them in the dumpster. And there was this old bag. I lifted it, and started to throw it out, and then I thought, *No, I'm going to look inside this one.* So I picked it up and opened it, and there was another bag inside, *and it was a bag of coins!* We always liked Pippi Longstocking—in fact, we were calling ourselves the "Pippi Longstocking Collective," or "Sisters of Pippi Longstocking"—so I said, "I found my treasure!" And we all sort of gathered around to look. It was mostly quarters, some half-dollars.

There was a long discussion, 'cause I wasn't sure, was it right to keep it? Or not? And then finally, I just gave in: "I guess it's okay. This was a gift to me." And so I took it, and I tucked it away somewhere. I guess I thought it must be worth something.

It moved with me several times, that bag of coins, and it ended up in Vermont, in the half school bus, underneath a bed that I had made. For months it would be just sitting under there. And years later, when I needed money to move my cabin, it suddenly dawned on me: *That's how I can afford to move my cabin. I have this treasure!*

I knew this guy Denis. He was a collector. And so I said to him, "You know, I have a bag of coins," and he said, "Bring them to me." So I brought them, and I dumped all the coins out on the table. He looked at them for ten, fifteen minutes. Then he picked up a coin, it was a silver dollar, and he said, "For this silver dollar, I'll go online, and I will sell your coins. And I'll do the best I can." He was quite sick at the time. I didn't know how sick. And I said, "Why only that coin?" And he said, "Because I know you don't have another one of these, and this coin is probably worth five hundred dollars." And I said, "I'm going to find another one like that in there!" And he just laughed. 'Cause there wasn't another one like that there. He knew.

So I left my coins with him, and he got me, I think, not quite two thousand dollars for that bag of coins. He said he was sorry: he just didn't have the energy to do better. But he got me that money.

And that was enough to pay for moving the cabin.

Gemma: Shoplifting

I BECAME AN EXPERT SHOPLIFTER in college. I had met a guy who did that, and he gradually taught me how to steal, and I became, I'd say, almost addicted to it. I'd feel this incredible freedom, like, "I can go in the store and get any book I want, or any piece of clothing." Most of it I gave away.

I remember going to Marshall Field's in Chicago, and walking out holding this eighty-dollar bathrobe, and just sitting outside laughing, how easy it had been.

Finally—two things stopped me. One, I got caught at Saks Fifth Avenue. They took my picture and they grabbed me. It was very scary, but I was also an actress, and I knew I had to act. So I cried, and said, "I'll never do this again! This is my first time ever!" And that was a lie. I had stolen from Saks Fifth Avenue several times before. And certainly in many, many other places. But they let me go.

Later, I worked for a ski area, out in Colorado, and I figured out a way to steal from the ski area. And then I heard the Buddhist teachings. I went to this meditation with Joseph Goldstein and Jack Kornfield and they said something about not taking what isn't freely offered, and it just pierced my heart. Like I just got it. And I never stole like that again.

And even today, if somebody steals something from me, I just think of it as karma being repaid. I just think, *I took plenty, so . . . let the retribution come in this lifetime.*

Stolen!

I HAD MONEY STOLEN ONCE. That was so disorienting. I was about to fly off to Minneapolis, and I went into a Starbucks, getting coffee. I reached into my purse and the wallet was gone. I'd had it hanging on the chair, and someone had just walked past and—the chaos that that created in the next twenty-four hours!

I had to go home, get my passport, drive back to the airport. And I remember all weekend, the panic of, *Where's my*

94

money? Where's my money? I called right away to get the credit card canceled, but my naïveté was that I didn't call the bank and get the account frozen. Whoever took it, just started writing checks. And nobody looked to check the handwriting. *Nobody!* So he emptied out the checking account just buying things, until I, I think on Monday, thought, *Well, maybe I should . . .* It was a real wake-up call for me. It really made me think about that purse and its contents and that sense of security.

I remember when my mom was quite ill towards the end with Parkinson's, she'd be calmed down when we would give her her purse. And I understand that. We have our identities in there, in relation to our access to money. So when my wallet was stolen, there was a loss of identity, just for that short time.

The Poor Box

YOU KNOW HOW THEY PASS the collection plate in church? My sister and I would take a handful, and then on the way out, we'd put it in the poor box. 'Cause the poor box never had any money in it. You know, it would have *coins*. And we would see the collection plate go down the aisle, and there were dollar bills in it. So we thought the poor box should have some dollar bills!

We never took any. We didn't steal it.

Roberta Hood

I WORKED IN A CREDIT OFFICE—there were these little charge plates they'd bring in. You'd buy something in the store, the clerk would make an imprint, she'd put it in a pneumatic tube, it would go *up up up!* and somebody else would collect the slips, and they'd be filed alphabetically by name. Everything was handwritten. "One pair of leather gloves—two dollars, fifty-five cents." "A bottle of perfume, a dress, a baby carriage." The slips would go in a heavy drawer, and then I'd carry them into a little teeny room filled with about eight or nine very big women, who were racketing away on these keypunching machines. They'd write up the bills, add them up, whatever.

But then, customers would send us letters about how they couldn't pay their bills. And it was my job to answer them. There'd be either a pink or a blue slip. "Urgent, we're going to have to cancel your card," or "You're going to a collection agency, or *errgh errgh errgh errgh.* . . ." So I'd read this stuff, and I'd feel terrible for these people. And when no one was looking I would take the paper and throw it away, hide it, put it in my pocket.

Once in a while, they'd write back, "I don't know *why* I didn't get my bill." And I'd go, "Uh-oh, I'm going to get in trouble!" I probably threw out many thousands of dollars. I was like Robin Hood, Roberta Hood, whatever.

And that was my relationship to money.

Outrageous Money

MONEY CAME SO EASILY TO people in the eighties. The eighties and part of the nineties. You had your drug money. Money that was outrageous money. Prostitution money. Alimony money.

I had a client that came—a lovely person—and she was terrified because she'd gotten caught embezzling from her job, forged checks, taken money. She was going to trial, and she wanted to know what the outcome would be: should she skip town or whatever. I'm not going to say what I advised her to do. [Gestures, "*Skip town!*"]

So she took out her checkbook to pay me, and of course that check bounced. There was no money in the account, and it probably wasn't even in her name. I started to laugh already because I knew.

And out she went, out the door, and I never heard from her again.

---

8. *Lies, Secrets & Silence*: Among Americans who have combined their finances with their spouse's, 31 percent say they have lied to their partners about money, and 58 percent admitted they hid cash. In addition, 15 percent hid a secret bank account, 11 percent lied about their debts, and 11 percent lied about how much money they earn. ForbesWoman/Harris Interactive, *The Week*, January 28, 2011.

INHERITANCE

*It's awfully hard for anybody to think money is money
when there is more of it than they can count.*

—Gertrude Stein

"ALTHOUGH WE RARELY SPEAK OF MONEY," writes Kate Levinson, "money is always talking—between spouses, partners, colleagues . . . children . . . parents . . . even strangers."[9] But for the children of inherited wealth, that voice can be exceptionally hard to hear. "Growing up, we never spoke about it," says the Quaker philanthropist Lydia Richardson Pratt. "I didn't know, for years, that we were the wealthiest people in town." Nor was she alone in her perplexity. "Nobody talked about it," says another, younger woman, who inherited a million dollars at the age of twenty-one. Her mother admits they did a terrible job preparing her: "We didn't help you figure it out at all."

Funny Money

MOST OF US FIRST ENCOUNTERED MONEY in a handful of coins, or some curiously inscribed paper, "This note is legal tender for all debts, public and private." Gradually, we came to recognize its potency in a handwritten check, a plastic credit card. These days, we watch it shift from screen to screen without ever materializing—a spatter of electronic impulses zipping invisibly through the ether.

But money has taken many other forms over the years.

A fine young horse, a herd of cattle, a string of cowry shells.
Wampum, made from seashells, white or black.
Dogs' teeth, porpoise teeth, the tusks of boars.
Tobacco, woolen blankets, cotton, pepper, salt.

Red feathers, beaver skins, the hides of rare white deer.
Human slaves, human skulls. Five sacks of rice.
Spices from the Orient. Muscovado sugar.
Lead bullets, wire, knives. A brand-new axe.

Dried cod, fresh coconuts, powdered indigo.
Silver ingots, diamonds, emeralds, pearls.
A ball of opium, a chest of pirate gold.
Polished mahogany, a case of whiskey.

A carton of American cigarettes.

The root of *credit* is the Latin *credo*, "I believe."
If we believe in money, it shouldn't matter what form it takes.

At school in England in the 1960s, money was Mars bars.

In the U.S., some systems use *time dollars* as a medium of exchange.

The stone discs of the Yap people,
huge wheels of close-grained white limestone,
are too heavy even to lift.

↞

Lydia: Old Money

MY NAME IS LYDIA RICHARDSON PRATT. And I like my name—very much. Last week I was rehearsing for a new play. And when we introduced ourselves, I, for some reason, said, "Lydia Richardson Pratt," and one of the other actors said, "Ah! That certainly sounds like an old money name."

I didn't say anything, but he knew. He had to know he'd hit the nail on the head. Oh, I got a kick out of that!

I was so ignorant that if anybody outside of my parents or my friends, if they implied anything or treated me differently, I didn't know. I mean, *o-bli-vi-ous!*

You wouldn't have known we were in a Depression. I was born in 1931, and that's pretty close to the Depression. But they weren't affected by it.

Daddy was a doctor. But it was Mummy who had the money. The Pratt Institute? That's my family. Daddy made normal money being a doctor. She made—she *had*—abnormal money, God bless her. Oh God! Pangs of guilt, but much joy!

It sounds so simple: *the money comes in and you give it out, so why worry?* But a lot of things are not as simple as they look. Like I thought I could help people, friends, because I didn't have to work for it. But it's just so emotional. You know, I didn't—you just have to learn these things as you go along.

The neat thing was, our mother gave to things we loved, like Planned Parenthood, the American Friends Service Committee. But I think she felt guilty about it. I *really* do. She did wonderful things with her money. But I think there was a reason, some kind of reason, that she *never* talked about it.

And Daddy—he didn't talk about it either.

So I never mentioned it till years later, when I was in analysis. We spent some time talking about money, Nathan and I. Not a lot, but enough. And Nathan was great. Oh, he was super. He was a Jungian analyst and he never made you feel guilty about anything. He didn't give two hoots that I was lesbian. *Did not give two hoots.* In fact, he kind of enjoyed it.

But it's funny. The women's movement helped me in every way except money. I remember I went to Haymarket. They had a conference for women who had money, and by then, I was just—just beginning to feel comfortable about being lesbian, so I realized I could talk about that.

But money—that was a secret.

They wanted us to say how much we had—and I had to quickly add up whatever the hell my income was. Everyone had to say, *out loud,* and I was probably one of the least rich, which sort of made it easier. I was so thankful I was last, so that I could get myself—a little bit get myself together. Everybody had big fat bucks. There were a couple of women who were Seagram Seven. *Big, big*-time stuff. So that was like *whoa-ho*!

In 1980, I probably had $80,000 a year. Which means that the principal was about four million. But coming out as lesbian was way easier than coming out as rich.

Some women hate me because I have money. I can feel it. I'm not going to try and analyze them. But they just don't like me.

Jilly and I were an item for five years, and she didn't come from money at all. I think it confused her. She would make little remarks once in a while that were not kindly. Little jabs.

And you know Miriam? Well, she's someone I just know doesn't like me. She's struggled for everything in her life, and everything's peaches and cream for me, so [she thinks] "Fuck her!" I mean, I can put myself into her shoes—mean, jealous—that's not very difficult. But it varies. Some people don't give a shit. Everybody is so different.

But I think it's smart not to talk about money. I'll tell you, and other people know, and that's fine. But I'm not going to be quote "out" about money. I don't think it's anybody's business. Because it does set people off. In one way or another. Just per se.

But the fact is that I love it. I can live like I want to. I can give like I want to. That's just a fucking thrill! Really, how many people can do that?

> *Privilege is my daily bread, and my minimum expectation is that I will have the maximum.*
>
> —Sam Keen

Phyllis: The Hoarder's Daughter

WHEN I WALKED INTO HIS HOUSE, I felt like I'd walked into the brain of somebody with mental illness. That's absolutely how it felt. I thought, *I am inside the brain of mental illness.*

My father was born during the Depression: working class, Polish, second generation. His biological mother was from Warsaw, but she died when he was eleven, twelve. Then his father remarried, and there were seven or eight kids in that blended family, and he kind of got lost. And his father was really hard on him. There was some rejection—deep rejection—there.

So he was a self-made man. He really saw himself as pulling himself up by his bootstraps. He started by picking dumps, and was able to turn that into cash, and his dad made soap, so he was part of a soap business, and later he went into the merchant marine and became an air-conditioning refrigeration mechanic. He was a fur trapper and trader, he was an auctioneer, a flea-marketeer, a buyer-seller, a wheeler-dealer, and eventually he hoarded money, and invested money, and that's where some of his wealth came from. But he lived in squalor, so . . . I had *no* idea. I thought he had delusions of grandeur.

When I was a kid, my dad was always rehabbing things. He bought this big old farmhouse, and we lived in four little rooms at the top, and he was always rehabbing all the other rooms. And he was an antique dealer. So it didn't look like hoarding. It looked like a hardworking man trying to make a living. But he didn't ever share that money. There was never enough money, never enough food. We didn't have a lot of heat in our home. You could take a shower once a week. There were real stringent guidelines around the spending of *anything*.

But you know, he bought that farm, and it was a farmhouse, five barns, and eighty acres, for twelve thousand dollars. And even in the seventies, that was considered a huge deal.

After I grew up, he never let me in the house. You'd go to the house, knock on the door, he'd open it a creak, look out, and say, "I'll be right down."

I remember picking up a piece of trash in his yard, and saying, "You need to clean this up before you die," and I held this thing up, and I said, "Like this! What is this?" He's like, "Well, if you didn't have your goddamn head up your ass, you'd know that that was worth something." And I remember saying, "Dad, it was maybe worth something at some point, but now it's *trash*." He was like, "Well, it could be used for this, or this, or this, or this!"

But he had a whole lot of trash. So when I did finally walk into his home, I really, literally dropped to my knees and I wept when I saw the condition he'd been living in.

He'd burned to death in the bathroom. He falls, he hits his head, he grabs something—it falls—whatever he grabs falls on top of him, there's a heater, an old heater, it falls, and the whole thing goes into flames. So when I walked in, the whole house was full of smoke.

The firefighters had called my brother and had him come to the house to help them search, because they had no idea where to look for the body, or even if he was home. But his car was in the driveway and there were no tracks leading out. The firefighters had to break all the windows to let out the smoke. And then it was winter, so they immediately had to put plywood up on all the windows, with these little teeny peek-holes to let in some light.

So I walk into this house, and it's just wall-to-wall filth and garbage and clothes and piles of papers and books and trash. By that time my brother and sister had already been working a day. They'd made enough space for me to walk about. So I looked to the left where the bedroom was, and there was about three and a half feet of clothing in that room. Clothing and pillows and lamps and pictures and chairs, kind of piled up, that you had to walk on it to get through. And there was a teeny little aisle through this hallway into the rest of the living area, and then a living-room-kitchen-dining-room area. Very, very small.

I look at it now, and I see a pile of trash. But really, it was layers of stuff. I wish I had taken a square foot, and done an inventory, because it would have been fascinating. It could be books and broken antiques and food and clothing, and a computer might be in there somewhere. Or a television. In the kitchen we found, like, twenty bags of hardened sugar, twenty five-pound bags. I opened the refrigerator, and there were probably three hundred packets of ketchup, mustard, and relish. And mayonnaise. Like, there wasn't anything in the refrigerator but that kind of shit.

I don't even know *what* there was. But I do know we wore Tyvek suits and headlamps, and masks over our faces, because it was so filthy and moldy and dirty. How do you clean? You can't. And it was freezing cold. 'Cause there was no heat.

It was a fifteen-room farmhouse, the attic and the basement included. All the outside, five barns, one of them was two floors. The ten-room motel across the street. The garage across the street. Then we got a call about the five-room summer house. And he had a trailer in the middle of the woods on Lake George in upstate New York. It just went *on and on and on and on and on.*

But it was unbelievable how fast we cleaned it up. My brother just went at it, every day, for months. I was in art school, so I'd drive to Boston, live there half the week, come home, get my work clothes, go all weekend, work, like twelve-fourteen-hour days, 'cause you know, we're Polish, we know how to work.

It took six months. . . .

↩

My dad had said to us, "If you want anything from me, you're going to have to work for it. You're going to have to look through everything, because I have money hidden everywhere." And he did.

I'd be cleaning out a drawer, and I'd find, you know, like five thousand dollars in one-hundred-dollar bills. Or under a rug, another five thousand dollars. There was a safe, no combination. I don't know how much cash was in there, but a fair amount. You might be cleaning something out, and you'd just find two hundred, or four hundred, or five hundred, or—ten thousand. It was, literally, everywhere. And not in any of the places you would think.

He used to say to me, "If you're good, you'll get a lot of money when I die, 'cause I'm a multimillionaire." And I'm like, "Yeah right!" Like, "Dad, you live in squalor." He's like, "I'm a multimillionaire, you have no idea."

He was! Yeah, I got half a million dollars.

I had a very estranged relationship with him. But just before he died, we actually reconciled to some degree. I'd go and visit. He'd peek out the door, and be, "I'm coming right out." And I'd take him to his church. I'd say, "Let's make a prayer for you." And he would bring me to Mother Mary. And I'd be like, "Mother Mary? I *love* Mother Mary!" And I'd say, "Let's make a prayer together." I was thinking we'd make up some prayer. And he starts saying the Hail Mary. And I'm like, "Okay!"

And I took him to the Skete Community, which is a community of monks up on a hill, near where he grew up. We arrived after Mass one day, you could still smell the incense in the church; we walked around this beautiful land and these beautiful buildings and just connected on this very spiritual level. And he's like, "Let me take you out to lunch. I have two coupons to Popeyes." And we'd go to Popeyes, so he'd be able to garner us two meals for under seven dollars with his coupons, and of course he'd take the pickle relish and the ketchup and the mustard with him.

But I saw him trying to connect, and open up to me in a way he never had in all my life before. So I can only hold it as a spiritual path. And that my being born to him was also my spiritual path. I think his life was a sacrifice for mine. It was a fast track to a generous soul, and to waking up, and to being all that I am.

As I was going though his stuff, I felt I needed to transform it. *And I thought, I'm going to make altars. They're going to be A-L-T-E-R A-L-T-A-R-S. Alter altars.* And so I started making altars. And I like the ones I've made.

I also took all of the objects from Africa that I could find, and I wrapped them in red cloth, and I sent them to all of the people I knew of African descent. I don't know what their value was, but they were beautiful. And everybody I knew got something in the mail.

Because my dad had mental illness, and was so abusive—it's really hard to see him in the light. But I'm trying to shift that now. I think he did the best he could. I think he cared deeply enough to hoard that money and distribute it, unevenly, but distribute it, to his children.

That money changed my life. It's very unusual, to go from a working-class to an upper-middle-class life. I've been able to travel, to support people I love to do the things they want to do. I put my niece through college in Columbia. I redid my kitchen. I've been able to make repairs on my house.

So, I think that that continues the transformation. And it is my belief that my dad is really happy; if there's any part of him left that's looking at me from the other side, that he's saying, "Yes! Good! I tried, and I didn't do so great. But I'm so glad you're able to do it on my behalf."

And you know, to have more compassion for his brokenness. . . .

←

Figuring It Out

I DON'T THINK I UNDERSTOOD we had money until quite late in the game, maybe high school. Friends would come by and they'd be floored that I lived in so big a house as I did—and on some level, it was shocking to me too. I had to go back and reframe: "Oh yeah, all those things would mean you have a lot of money." But nobody talked about it.

It was probably taboo from the generation before.

At some point, they told me this money was coming. I was shocked, stunned. I had absolutely no idea what it meant.

My mother says, "We did a terrible job preparing you. We didn't help you figure it out at all."

How much? I think it was a million.

My money was originally managed by the man who managed my father's money, and I wanted to move it. And that was a fight! A woman-powered fight. Because that man was my father's cousin, sort of an uncle-esque figure, and everything was being mailed to my father. I asked him [the guy] some questions, and he basically said. "Don't worry your pretty little head over it."

At which point I thought, *I cannot be in this situation!* It was just so infantilizing. So that was a little moment of revolt.

Iron Fist

I HAVE THIS CLIENT WHO INHERITED twenty-five million dollars, and her husband blew through all of it, brought the family business into bankruptcy. He asked his wife to bail him out, and he lost her money too. But she has absolutely learned her lesson. When her husband was going through the courts, and they were almost ruined, her lawyer said to her, *"Don't you ever—don't you ever give your husband your money again."*

So she squirrels away money like you would not believe. The most elegant French lady. She's just so pretty and so well-spoken and lovely. But the financial stress has been enormous. And she has . . . taken over. She was not trained to do any of that. She sat with the accountant. They went line by line through every single bill that came in. The magazine subscriptions *went*, the country club memberships *went*. It was fascinating to watch her—once she got over the shock—just completely take control. And now she says, "David's lovely, but he still thinks that money grows on trees!"

And she handles their finances with an iron fist, because she never wants to go to that place again.

Frozen Assets

I USED TO MANAGE MONEY for a woman in Connecticut— clearly the black sheep in her family. She'd be in her nineties by now. But she came from this fancy family in Philadelphia, and someone died, and she was left a couple of million dollars. The bank called her up and told her she was inheriting this money, and they kept saying, "Where should we transfer the money? Where should we mail the stock certificates, *blah, blah, blah?*" And she said, "Send them all to me." Because *she wanted to see what a million dollars looked like.*

And what did she do with all the envelopes? She put them in the freezer!

Because if your house burns down, your freezer is protected, so she felt that that was safer than the safe. So she put her million dollars' worth of stock certificates in the freezer!

Bottomless

THE MONEY WAS ALWAYS THERE. It never occurred to me to be worried about it. And I gave it away all the time. My friend Jess called me. I woke up in the middle of the night, the phone ringing: "I'm in jail in Laramie, I just shot a cow thinking it was a moose, and I've been put in jail, and I need five hundred dollars to get out." I mailed her five hundred dollars the next morning. And it never occurred to me to worry about getting it back. I had no sense there was ever going to be an end to it. Like, I'd take five or six people out to dinner and never even think about it.

I think it was a combination of feeling it was bottomless, and *feeling like it was the reason for all the pain.*

9. "Although we rarely speak of money . . .": Kate Levinson, *Emotional Currency: A Woman's Guide to* Building *a Healthy Relationship with Money* (Berkeley, CA, Celestial Arts, 2011).

GIVING IT AWAY

Money can buy happiness, if we spend it on other people.
—H. H. the Dalai Lama & Archbishop Tutu

SOME WOMEN KEEP SPENDING till there's nothing left, as if to strip themselves of the guilt and the bewilderment, the daunting overwhelm of their inheritance. Others learn how to stand up for themselves, taking pleasure in their own good fortune, and at the same time finding ways to share it, delighting in the opportunities this opens up. My friend Phyllis, the "Hoarder's Daughter," inherited half a million dollars after her father died. "That money changed my life," she says. "I've been able to travel, to support people I love to do the things they want to do."

Another friend with inherited wealth has very consciously taken on the role of philanthropist. The first time someone asked her for a particular donation at a higher level[10] than she had imagined possible, she was stunned. "But what a gift! Because it helped me put myself in context, and I don't know that I could have done that by myself. Not that I wouldn't have wanted to be generous, but because, *who knew?*"

⤺

Clary: Money Magic

MY NAME IS CLARY SAGE, and I'm a psychic by profession, which means that people come to see me, they sit at my table, and I read the tarot cards and tell them about whatever I see: their future, their past, their present, and whatever's going on. I've been a reader, what? Forty years? That's a lot of readings, thousands.

Last week I had two princesses, the mother and the daughter. *Princesses!* They came from a palace and I have a bathtub in the kitchen—and still they climb the stairs. But their money could never buy what I know and who I am. There's a card in the tarot deck called the five of pentacles. It shows two people walking past a church, two beggars in the snow. Many wealthy people pick that card, and I know that they have nothing. They're poor, yeah, poor in spirit. They have money—you can see the coins—but they're like beggars in the snow.

❦

My father had a restaurant in Buffalo, New York. The sports people came in, the midget wrestlers. It was a circus atmosphere for a child. Sometimes I'd go to work with him. He'd have bags and bags of change, and he'd have me sort out the pennies and the quarters, and you'd hear the money—that old trick they use in slot machines—that *ding-ding-ding!* I loved the ding of the dimes in my father's restaurant. I'd sit in the phone booth, feed in the dimes, and they'd go down.

114

Ding-ding! I love that sound.

And my dad made money magic. He got up very early to prepare the food for the breakfast customers, and he didn't come home till late at night. But he'd make patterns for us, on the table, with the change—not piles, but very elaborate designs. They were like mosaics with the copper pennies and the quarters and the nickels. So when I woke up, my father would be gone, but there'd be this money in intricate patterns on the table. And that was our allowance, for my brother, my sister, and me.

So I never had anxiety about money, not one day in my life. Never. Because my father taught me, *it will be there on the table.* And it is.

↤

I've had many clients—beautiful women, attractive, professional—who've come to ask me about possible husbands, wealthy husbands, for one reason only: *to get the alimony, to get a buyout or a property.* Sometimes I will counsel them about what they're doing. But in my readings, there are very few things I judge. I just try to open up and see.

But these are women who are looking for that man; for them it's a business move. They are going to stay in that marriage for a while, and then divorce. They show me photographs. And they want to know: *Are they going to be brutalized? Are they going to end up with the money?* They handpick these men. No different than looking for a sperm donor or going on match.com. They are young, very attractive women, and they are going after rich men, after billionaires. It's their body, it's their time put in. And many of the ones I've seen, later, they were able to accomplish it.

Some of these women were set up for life. Some also did get children. They wanted the children, they wanted the gene pool, they wanted the support and the college paid. Takes a lot. I mean, they really followed through.

> *Thirty percent of American women don't intend to stay with their husbands five years from now.*
> —Michael Silverstein

I encourage people who are in bad marriages, terrible marriages, to start buying jewelry, start hiding the money, start looking, find out what your husband has. I had a client who was going through a divorce, and she had no idea what her husband was worth. Never would look in the drawer. And she finds out he owns an airline, a department store, a vitamin company, and he's crying poverty! Oh, that really helped her. *Secrets, secrets, secrets!*

I've been doing readings since the seventies. In the early days, it was mostly about love. *Who will I meet, how many children?* Fortune-telling questions. The eighties brought the money questions. *Should I buy a condo? What about*

my job? They also brought health questions because of the AIDS crisis. But the two thousands and the middle to later part of the nineties brought something really new, which warmed my heart: *Philanthropy! Philanthropy,* which I never saw before. And then the crash and the crisis.

I had three clients—three!—who lost everything to Bernie Madoff. They called me—and I said, "Oh, oh, let's backtrack here. Did I ever tell you you were going to lose all your money?" And they said, "Well, yes, you started to. You said, 'Oh, I see this guy, he's like your grandfather, your uncle, and I don't like what he's doing with your money, you should look into it.'" And they all said, "No, Clary, you must be wrong. We're *making* money." And you know, if you interrupt me and you say, "Oh no, you're wrong," I let it go.

And I'm sorry, looking back, who could know? I mean, it's crazy now. Money's gone whack-a-doo. *Whack-a doo!*

So we went from the people who were giving it away to the ones who were being humbled by losing a lot. I have the chills telling you this. *Money did change, you know.* So many people coming to see me, even the ones who lost their jobs, they want to help others in some way. They were thinking, *Well, maybe I'll volunteer, take a lesser job, but help someone else pull herself up.*

So that touches my heart. Different than how much more can I make or get. Like my father taught me, the money will be there on the table. And it is.

❦

Thirty-one percent of Americans who have combined their finances with their spouses' say they have lied to their partners about money. Fifty-eight percent admitted they hid cash. Fifteen percent hid a secret bank account, eleven percent lied about their debts, and eleven percent lied about how much money they earn.

—ForbesWoman/Harris Interactive,
The Week, January 28, 2011

Carson: Microcredit

MY NAME IS CARSON. My specialty is microloans: lending very, very small sums of money to desperately poor people, most of them village women who have no collateral, and trusting them to pay it back.

Which they do! Women are, in fact, a far better credit risk than men.

I learned that when I was a little girl in Louisiana. My father was the last of the big-time spenders. He wanted to be the life of the party and buy everybody a round of drinks and act like he was rich and money was no problem. And my mom, meanwhile, had to be what she called "very Scottish" and tight. So he got to be the generous one, and she got to be the stingy one, because she had the responsibility for making it all work.

She had six of us to feed on a limited income. She'd get day-old bread from the bakery at half price, and freeze it.

She'd drive down to the coast, where the shrimp boats come in, and buy the shrimp right off the boat. Fruit she'd buy, but it was rationed. There were rules around what you could eat, what you couldn't, how much, and all of that. You could do unlimited cereal and bread. So Momma made sure we all had our tummies full, and then she'd divvy out the treats and more expensive things.

But she was very creative, so we never felt that we were lacking.

There's a photograph of me at five years old, serving my father bacon and eggs, using the beer tray as a server and wearing a little apron. I got quarters as tips. And when I was in first grade, maybe second grade, Mama opened a savings account, and we were encouraged to save.

In fifth grade I got my first real job. I was the first girl to be a newspaper carrier in my town. My brother had to be my front 'cause girls weren't allowed to be newspaper carriers then. You could do it after school, just roll the papers, and ride a bike around the neighborhood, and collect on weekends. And that was fabulous, 'cause it meant I could save my first $100 and—eventually—buy into my first car. "The maroon baboon with the banana fender," we called it. One of the fenders had been repaired, and it was yellow, bright yellow!

So money equaled transport, equaled freedom.

↵

My father was not going to pay for college 'cause I was "just going to get married anyway, and what's the point of education, and *blah, blah, blah . . .*" It makes me embarrassed for him now. So I told him, "Well, I'll pay for it myself!"

And in retrospect, I really had the little angels looking out for me! 'Cause how on earth would I get a break? But I earned tuition waitressing. Double shifts. Mornings at the Aloha Best Western and evenings at the Lobster House. And I lied to get those jobs. I said I had thirteen years' experience at Barb's Bar & Grill. Barbara is my mother's name. Sweet, right? But I'd been serving food and drinks since I was five years old.

And people are wonderful. People are generous. I always made great tips. So I worked hard, made all this money, had enough to pay my own tuition to Georgetown University, and from there went on to Harvard, and to Oxford.

The truth is, I'm still astonished by it all. . . .

↜

So, after Oxford I went to work for the Ford Foundation. They moved me to Bangladesh in the late 1980s, where I met Muhammad Yunus, the economist who invented microfinance. Very privileged perch: my job was to give away money in one of the poorest countries in the world.

I remember visiting this one woman, Khaleda, when her neighbor happened to stop by. You know, when a foreigner comes, everybody swarms around. And the kids are hanging 'round behind their mothers' saris and I'm trying to get a sense of who is who. Khaleda had only been in a borrowing group for a couple of years and her neighbor wasn't a member, I'm not sure why. And what was so dramatic was when they introduced me to their children. Khaleda's three-year-old was the size of her neighbor's six-year-old. And it was because of the stunting and wasting that goes on when kids don't have enough to eat. All of a sudden, I could see the differences right there. Those first six years of a child's life are so important. And I became just rabidly committed to trying to go as fast as possible, because you could see the cost of going slow in real human lives.

And the shock I had when I met a woman who for the last three days had eaten only—they have a term in Bangla for the water that you boil rice in—she'd been getting that from the neighbors. Or the little girl I encountered, her new husband was so excited, just been married—they brought me into the home to see her, this little lump in red, still in the red sari. I lifted up her veil. Just a child! Maybe thirteen, crying. It totally broke my heart and radicalized me.

So it was in Bangladesh that I realized I needed to be part of the women's movement, and that we needed to work for our own liberation and all others', 'cause—it's so unjust! And my recognition of my own wealth and privilege was very clear.

↫

More than half the population of the globe lives on less than $2.50 a day. Even in the U.S., in 2004, 30% of households has less than $12,000 in net worth. The bottom 90% owns only 29% in total net worth, with 34% going to the top 1%."

Juliet B. Schor

And years later, when Muhammad Yunus was awarded the Nobel Peace Prize, I immediately wanted to make sure that the full board came. Because nine of those twelve board members were village women, and that would be really incredible.

They picked Taslima Begum to join Yunus at the podium, and she was just so sweet and so adorable. She had used her loans to buy some goats, and she grew mangoes in her front yard that she harvested and sold. She left her husband home with their two boys as she takes her first airplane ride and jets over to Oslo, and then later they go on to London and Paris! I mean!

And on the day itself, when the hall was packed and the ceremony was in full swing, Taslima Begum comes out and stands on the stage, and she begins to speak in Bangla, and she says, "On behalf of poor women everywhere, I accept this prize. And I want to tell you that we're not going to stop, we're not going to stop working until all of us—all of us!—are out of poverty!"

It was just so moving. These were women who'd never slept in a proper bed or seen television before or used a Western toilet or a shower.

↬

But what I've learned is that whether you sleep on a mat on the floor or on a fancy mattress, it's still a bed, right? Same thing from the stool to the chair to the recliners and the lavish sofa. And that climb out of poverty onto a treadmill of more and more and more accumulation, all that is fine, let people be in that race to their hearts' content. But there needs to be a point below which people cannot fall. And that's where my interest has really been—to make sure everyone has at least some minimum level of enough. Being able to eat at least one meal a day, and once a week some protein, that's not a lot to ask. That's not three squares, you know.

So now my work, a lot of it, is raising resources. Poor people, rich people—everybody wants to give. 'Cause we've gotta have more money in women's hands, we've gotta have more money in hands that can control it and can use it for the improvement of their lives—and of their kids' lives too. Plus I would also argue for women's right to buy bangles!

So, that's the story. As Taslima said in Stockholm, "We're not going to stop till all of us—*all of us!*—are out of poverty!"

What a Gift!

THERE WAS AN ARTICLE IN THE LOCAL PAPER about people who give money away, and my husband and I were in it. I hadn't understood how prominently featured we'd be; we really were almost all of it. But coming out about money really is a coming out. My tenant said, "Oh, my gosh, everybody's asking me about it." And I said, "Well, *you'll* hear about it. Nobody's going to mention it to me." And it was true. Even once you've come out, people are a little shy to speak to you about it.

I don't belong in the top one percent. But when you Google yourself in the world, you can't believe how high you are. So many of us—even if we're not high in this country, we're high in the world. And that's a good thing to hold on to, when you're feeling like "*Well, I can' t have...*" Like, what do I mean, "I can't ..." like, *hello*! The world can't have heat, and I'm complaining. You know, that's helpful.

The first time somebody actually asked me for money for good works, at a level that was beyond what I imagined I could give, I was stunned! But what a gift! Because it helped me put myself in context, and I don't know that I could have done that by myself. Not because I wouldn't have wanted to be generous, but because, *who knew?*

⤙

> *Women are on the whole more generous than men, giving away some 3.5 percent of our income, as compared to men's 1.8 percent.*
>
> —Debra Mesch

Singing & Dancing

WE COULD HAVE PLASTERED THE REFRIGERATOR with Mom's sayings. *Can I think of them now?* About money, "You're always rich if you have enough to share."

Everybody in my family grew up with that.

My mother had these two friends, Maura and Louise. Maura was right off the boat from Ireland, she worked in the convent doing laundry for the nuns, and Louise was very black—I remember that, coal black. Growing up Irish, everybody's got this pink and white skin, and Louise had this beautiful, smooth, shiny, almost bluish-black skin. I remember always wanting to feel it. She cleaned houses for the rich folk. And the three of them were always singing and laughing and dancing. They were making cookies, they were sewing things, they were getting donations, "for the poor folk." And they had a ball!

It's by spending oneself that one becomes rich.
—Sarah Bernhardt

The Two Paintings

IT WAS MY MOTHER WHO SHOWED ME how to be a philanthropist. She just did it very nicely, and I could see the pleasure she received from it.

Yeah, it was my mother. I picked that up from her.

There were two paintings I gave away, a Winslow Homer, and a Whistler, "Pretty Nellie Brown." Both of them I'd grown up with. Suddenly a lot of drugs came into the area. I was at the Co-op, and a woman who worked there said they'd taken her whole safe. And I said, "I gotta get rid of those paintings. I have to get rid of them." And, oh God, that was so hard. I loved the Whistler. I just—*wow!*

But pretty soon after that, I knew who I wanted to give them to: the Pennsylvania Academy of the Fine Arts in Philadelphia, and the big art museum in Philadelphia. So I gave the Whistler to the Pennsylvania Academy of the Fine Arts.

They hadn't had a Whistler oil. And I gave it, I did not sell it. But the head of the trustees, the letter he wrote me was just so beautiful—it was the opposite of crass. It was loving! Just so loving! So that was great.

A woman came with her boyfriend to pick it up. They didn't want some moving company. She'd never seen the painting before, of course, and very early on, she said, "This must really be hard for you." Oh, and I burst into tears! And she called me up that night, about ten o'clock, and said, "I just wanted you to know your painting is safe in the vault." Oh, it was just—that whole experience was so great.

With the big museum, it was a whole different thing. I called and asked to speak to the people who took care of watercolors, and I say, "This is Lydia Richardson Pratt. You don't know me, but I have a Winslow Homer watercolor that I'd like to give to you." And the woman's first response was—this was not the curator, I can assure you. Her first response was, "Well, is it in good shape?" And I said, "Madam, I would not be giving you this painting if it were not in good shape."

I didn't realize until later, that everybody gives *crap*.

So, then a big truck came up. *Grhrhrhrh* . . . And that year just happened to be the museum's 125th anniversary. So of course, I get an invitation, and I say my name, and the woman says, "Oh, you have to follow me." So we go upstairs to the woman who is the curator—she's so cute, she's so fucking cute! And she takes me to see the painting, shows me where it is. They've cleaned it up, and it just looks gorgeous. And she says, "This is the most beautiful Winslow Homer we have in the collection." And then she says, "You know, we're always soliciting paintings and money, and then somebody comes along out of the blue and gives us a Winslow Homer!" She just couldn't get over it. And that's 'cause both those pictures were just absolutely superb.

But that's how I was brought up. That gives you an indication of the generosity of my mother.

Moving to Austin

I HAVE ANOTHER STORY OF GENEROSITY that has always stuck with me. It's about my daughter, Sara. She was twenty-one years old, independent, supporting herself, working at a restaurant in town. And she was waiting on a woman who was a regular. They were just sort of chatting with each other. The woman was asking her about herself. And Sara said, "Well, I'm moving to Austin, I'm taking off in a few weeks, and you know it's a little challenging."

She was just telling her her story.

And when this woman paid her bill—she was on her own, she probably had like a twenty-five-dollar meal ticket—she gave Sara all the cash she had on her. Which was—several hundred dollars. She said, "I want you to have this cash for your new life." And Sara was like, "What! You don't even know me." She said, "I am just really moved by your story."

She gave her three or four hundred dollars to help with the move.

The Silver Dollar

EVERY SUNDAY, BEFORE WE WENT off to Niagara Falls, we'd go to visit my grandfather. We'd sit on the porch swing, my sister and I, and out would come my Italian grandfather who didn't speak English—his hands Parkinson-shaking—and he'd give us each a silver dollar, and it was like, "Oh, magic!"

We'd sit together on that cold iron porch swing, and he'd say, "*Shh*, don't tell anybody!" and we'd go *"Oooh!"*

It was a big coin, and it was shiny, round and silver like the moon.

Deepest Wish

Money has got to disappear from the scene to make me happy.
I wish we were back with barter. That would be such a cool system.

My own deepest wish?
I wish to have a lot of money—make a lot of money—
so that I can provide the comfort life for my children.

A quarter of a million dollars would change our lives forever.
But twenty thousand would be nice this week too.

Because you're rich, you're going to go to school and get a nice job,
and succeed at most everything you do.
But give us, the poor ones, give *us* a chance.
Give *us* money, and see what we do with it.

I just want some guy to take care of all my fucking problems.
But how can I say that?

Rich people are tormented,
Middle-class people are tormented, poor people are tormented.
I wish more of us could just appreciate the amount we have.

I would like it to be experienced as energy,
like sunlight and water and firewood.
That's what I'd like: *for money to be more transparent.*

I don't want to be rich.
Well, I could take being rich, I guess.
But that's not my goal.
My goal is to be comfortable and not worry about it.

I wish that money could *shrink.*
I'd like to take a magical wand and go *"Psssssssh . . .*
Go back down, to the size of a piece of paper,
instead of swelling to this false god,
the size of a movie screen,
that we all have to pay such fraught attention to."

---

10. *Giving It Away*: Debra Mesch, "The Gender Gap in Charitable Giving: Studies Show That Women Are More Likely to Donate Than Men, and to Donate More." *The Wall Street Journal*, February 1, 2016.

CODA

Money Prayers

FOR THOSE WHO PAUSE A MOMENT before reaching for the bill. For those who *save-and-save-and-save-and-save*, and never have enough. For those who put a dime inside each shoe, hoping to walk towards sufficiency. For those who are, as they say, "comfortable," meaning they are safe, they have abundance; they have guilt. For those who take a five-dollar bill, a ten, a twenty, and squirrel them away around the house. For those who lie and practice subterfuge. For those who shop for Christmas presents at Goodwill. For those who follow stocks and bonds each day. For those who just don't care. For those who panic, who can't bear to look at their bank statements. For those who speak openly about such things. For those who are embarrassed to speak. For those who say, in all honesty, "I don't know anybody who has less than me." For those who push past terror in order to be generous. For those with absolutely nothing left. For all whose heads bow down like windblown corn beneath the great god, Money.

MONEY QUESTIONS

→ *What is your name? When and where were you born? What is your current job or work identity? If you had to place yourself in terms of class, where would you put yourself? Is it the same as the class into which you were born?*

→ *What did you learn about money growing up? How did your parents deal with money (father, mother, older relatives)? Who made the financial decisions? Was any of this kept secret? For some people, there's a lot of shame attached to the subject of money. Was this in any way true for you? How was this affected by class, religion, conscious values, if at all?*

→ *What was your first job? How old were you then? Do you remember how much it paid?*

→ *What was the most satisfying purchase you ever made? The most expensive? Do you remember how much it cost?*

→ *Do you have a story about something you longed for which then proved to be a disappointment?*

→ *Do you feel you were raised to feel "competent" with money* in practical terms? If not, how did you educate yourself? Are there places of awkwardness or ignorance even now? Have you ever felt frightened or anxious in relation to money? With whom do you talk most freely?

→ What work have you done over the course of your life? What did you learn from these various jobs? Do you have any money stories having to do with work?

→ Do you feel that your relationship to money differs from that of the men in your life? From your father or your brothers, your male friends? How has this changed over the years?

→ Do you have any stories about women supporting other women in relationship to money?

→ Have you any examples of exceptional generosity in relationship to money? On your own part or on the part of someone else?

→ Have you ever experienced any unexpected windfalls?

→ Have you any stories of startling losses or betrayals having to do with money?

→ What is your own biggest money issue at the moment?

→ Do you know anyone who has a really calm, sane, sweet relationship to money? What do you admire about the way that person handles things?

→ *Do you have any private habits or rituals having to do with money? Do you have any particular places where you like to economize or be extravagant? What does "enough" mean to you?*

→ *What is your favorite story about money? Do you remember any sayings, any fairy tales or parables? Are there any that seem especially true to you right now?*

→ *If you had to explain the role of money in today's world, how would you describe it?*

→ *What attitudes/actions/resources would you turn to if the economy should continue to worsen? What does "safety" look like to you?*

→ *What is your deepest wish in relation to money? Mark Slouka writes that there might be buried under our assumptions "another system of value." What might that look like to you?*

→ *Is there anything you'd like to add?*

BIBLIOGRAPHY

Atwood, Margaret. Payback: *Debt and the Shadow Side of Wealth* (Toronto, ON, Anansi Press, 2012).

Buchan, James. *Frozen Desire* (New York, Farrar, Straus, & Giroux, 1997).

Ehrenreich, Barbara. *Nickel and Dimed: On (Not) Getting By in America* (New York, Metropolitan Books, Henry Holt, 2001).

Ferguson, Niall. *The Ascent of Money: A Financial History of the World* (New York, Penguin Press, 2008).

Hyde, Lewis, *The Gift: Imagination and the Erotic Life of Property* (New York, Vintage Books, 1983).

Kristof, Nicholas D., and Sheryl WuDunn. *Half the Sky: Turning Oppression into Opportunity for Women Worldwide* (New York, Alfred A. Knopf, 2009).

Levine, Judith: *Not Buying It: My Year Without Shopping* (New York, Free Press, 2006).

Levinson, Kate. *Emotional Currency: A Woman's Guide to*

Building a Healthy Relationship with Money (Berkeley, CA, Celestial Arts, 2011).

Lockhart, Russell, James Hillman, et al. *Soul and Money* (Dallas, Spring Publications, 1982).

Offill, Jenny, and Elissa Schappell, eds. *Money Changes Everything: Twenty-Two Writers Break the Final Taboo—How Money Transforms Families, Tests Marriages, Destroys Friendships, and Sometimes Manages to Make People Happy* (New York, Broadway Books, 2007).

Randall, Margaret. *The Price You Pay: The Hidden Cost of Women's Relationship to Money* (New York, Routledge, 1996).

Schor, Juliet B. *Plenitude: The New Economics of True Wealth* (New York, Penguin Press, 2010).

Tasch, Woody. *Inquiries into the Nature of Slow Money: Investing as if food, farms, and fertility mattered* (White River Junction, VT, Chelsea Green, 2008).

Twist, Lynne, with Teresa Barker. *The Soul of Money: Transforming Your Relationship with Money and Life* (New York, W. W. Norton, 2003).

RESOURCES

A Network for Grateful Living (ANGeL)
245 Russell Street, 21B
Hadley, MA 11035
www.gratefulness.org / contact@gratefulness.org

A Network for Grateful Living is a global organization offering online and community-based educational programs and practices that inspire and guide a commitment to grateful living, and catalyze the transformative power of personal and societal responsibility.

"We hold grateful living as an engaged mindfulness practice, grounded in both wisdom and science, which supports our ability to see the wonder and opportunity in every moment, and motivates us to act boldly with love, generosity, and respect towards one another, ourselves, and the Earth."

The Harnisch Foundation/Creative Philanthropy
599 Lexington Avenue, 46th floor
New York, NY 10022
212-904-0454
www.thehf.org / info@thehf.org

Identifies potential partners and cultivates relationships between large, fairly traditional donors interested in devoting more resources to social transformation, and projects that serve the health and welfare of the planet through social transformation and the interface between spirituality and social change. Gives awards to social visionaries, social entrepreneurs, and social activists. Believes in investing in storytellers and media makers.

Imagine Philanthropy
Julia Frost, Client Relations Team Lead
978-866-0208
www.imaginephilanthropy.com
Julia@ImaginePhilanthropy.com

Imagine Philanthropy is an international consulting firm that supports philanthropists in building effective giving strategies and guides organizations and nonprofit leaders seeking to enhance and energize their work.

Landmark Worldwide
353 Sacramento Street
San Francisco, CA 94111
415-981-8850
www.landmarkworldwide.com / info@landmarkworldwide.com

An international training and development company offering programs to empower participants to think and act beyond existing views and limits, and enhance personal productivity, organizational effectiveness, and communication.

The Ms. Foundation for Women
12 MetroTech Center, 26th floor
Brooklyn, NY 11201
212-742-2300
info@msfoundation.org

The Ms. Foundation works to bring attention to the challenges facing women, especially women of color and low-income women. It advocates for national and statewide policy change to address those challenges, meanwhile supporting more than 100 organizations that are working for change on a grassroots level. Recent grantees have focused on a wide range of issues, including health care and economic justice.

National Endowment for Financial Education (NEFE)
1331 17th Street, Suite 1200
Denver, CO 80202
303-741-6333
www.nefe.org

The National Endowment for Financial Education is a leading nonprofit foundation providing financial education and practical information, all at no cost to the consumer. NEFE believes strongly that, regardless of background or income level, all Americans can enjoy better, more secure and satisfying lives through an increased understanding of their own financial issues. It offers research and consumer surveys, financial education resources, and a host of other teaching materials, for people at every stage of life.

Proteus Fund
15 Research Drive, Suite B
Amherst, MA 01002
413-256-0349
www.proteusfund.org / info@proteusfund.org

In today's world, philanthropy for long-term systemic change must be reimagined to be more strategic than ever before. It's easy to set ambitious goals—but how do you make sure you're working with the right allies? How do you assess your progress? How do you know if you're building effective networks—and are they sustainable?

As a full-service philanthropy organization, Proteus Fund brings funders and movement leaders together to create the collaborative systems and strategies needed to create and protect enduring social change.

Rachel's Network
1200 18th Street NW, Suite 910
Washington, DC 20036
202-659-0846
www.rachelsnetwork.org / info@rachelsnetwork.org

Named in honor of Rachel Carson, Rachel's Network is a community of women funders committed to a safer, healthier, and more just world for all. Members occupy more than a hundred director positions on the boards of major environmental organizations and give close to $60 million a year combined—through personal and foundation grants and investments—for the benefit of our planet.

Kathy Lemay
Raising Change
245 Main Street, Suite 202
Northampton, MA 01060
www.raisingchange.com / info@raisingchange.com

Raising Change transforms philanthropy and giving, equipping individuals from all walks of life with tools to live and lead their most generous life, make a lasting difference, and positively influence the world's unwritten future.

"Our team blends a deep mix of boots-on-the-ground experience with marketing, finance, and technology to provide the most effective techniques in fund-raising and community building available today."

The Soul of Money Institute
3 Fifth Avenue
San Francisco, CA 94118
415-386-5599
www.soulofmoney.org / info@soulofmoney.org

The Soul of Money Institute provides transformational and educational programs that inspire and empower individuals, organizations, and institutions to:

Align the acquisition and allocation of their financial resources with their most deeply held values;

Move from an economy of fear, consumption, and scarcity, to an economy of sufficiency, sustainability, and generosity;

Generate an expanding flow of resources toward the affirmation of life and the common good; and

Enable people to relate to money and the money culture with greater freedom, power, and effectiveness.

Women Donors Network
565 Commercial Street, Suite 300
San Francisco, CA 94111
415-814-1333
www.womendonors.org / info@womendonors.org

This network of donors and donor activists provides opportunities for networking, leadership development, and peer support. It hosts a donor and study circle and a media circle, and gives away at least $25,000 per year.

Women's Funding Network
156 Second Street, 2nd floor
San Francisco, CA 94105
415-441-0706
www.womensfundingnetwork.org / info@womensfundingnetwork.org

WFN aims to bring together the financial power and influence of funders of gender equity in order to address and solve critical and complex social issues ranging from poverty to global security.

They strive to build a world where every woman and girl has the resources to achieve her full potential. Their guiding values are equality, partnership, transparency, diversity, and inclusion.

Women's Perspective
P.O. Box 244
Fairfield, CT 06824
203-243-2238
www.womensperspective.org / info@womensperspective.org

Women's Perspective offers educational opportunities that inspire women to integrate their economic and spiritual power for positive change in their own lives and the world.

"We believe that women bring a unique voice to the discussion of money, values, and economic resources. Since 1984, our workshops, retreats, and transformational trips have provided opportunities and inspiration for women to see money as a central dynamic of their spiritual journey. We encourage women to identify the ways money impacts their self-image, relationships, work and community involvement. By connecting their values to their financial decisions, women truly become the architects of their own lives and the world they live in."

ACKNOWLEDGMENTS

MULTITUDINOUS THANKS TO ALL THE WOMEN who let me interview them about their relationship to money, especially Edite Cunha, Susan Davis, Terry Iacuzzo, Phyllis Labanowski, Kathy O'Rourke, Verandah Porche, Jennifer Taub, and Linda Winston. Without you, this little book would not exist.

Thanks too to everyone who has supported my work over the years, in particular Susan Davis, Will Hurd, Jenny Ladd, and Ann Stokes, and to all the organizations that contributed funds or practical help, including Art Angels, the Astraea Foundation, the Five College Women's Studies Resource Center, the Puffin Foundation, and the Massachusetts Cultural Council.

Thanks to Verandah Porche, Jenny Ladd, and Rythea Lee, who helped coax my lengthy interviews into something resembling a play, and to all those who worked to stage the original production, especially Melissa Redwin, Pam & Rachel Hannah, Amy Pulley & Alice Cozzolino, and Phyllis Labanowski, and of course the performers themselves: Barbara Cortez-Grieg, Kris B., Vanessa Calderon, Danielle Connor, Sue Davis, Rachel Hannah, Louise Krieger, Rona Leventhal,

Trenda Loftin, Valorie Pennington, and Karen Sheaffer.

Thanks too to everyone who encouraged me and made me welcome as I began to carry Legal Tender out into the world, in particular Tuti Scott of Imagine Philanthropy; Eva Thomson of Thomson Financial Management; Pam Hannah at the UMassFive College Federal Credit Union; Rev. Jacqui Lewis at the Middle Collegiate Church in NYC; Steve Zeitlin at City Lore in NYC; John Bloom at RSF Social Finance in San Francisco; Kate Levinson, author of Emotional Currency; Katie Matney of the Women's Fund of Central Ohio; and Nancy Schwartz Sternoff of the Dobkin Family Foundation.

Thanks as always to my family back in the UK: my mother, Brigid McEwen; my sisters, Helena and Isabella; my brother, John; his wife, Rachel, and their family; and my beloved uncle Johnny.

Thanks too to my tribe of friends on this side of the Atlantic, especially Barbara Bash, Kathleen Bowen, Edite Cunha, Susan Davis, Ruth Gendler, Penny Gill, Janice Gould, Parker Huber, Annabel McCall, Maia, Pat Musick, Susie Patlove, Verandah Porche, Amy Pulley, Sarah Rabkin, Joy Seidler, Michelle Spark, Arthur Strimling, Davis Te Selle, Chris Ulrich, Paki Wieland and Linda Winston.

And finally, thanks to Annie Bissett for her gorgeous artwork, and to everyone at Bauhan Publishing for their steady kindness and hard work, in particular Sarah Bauhan, Mary Ann Faughnan, Jody Hetherington, Henry James, and Jocelyn Lovering.

In *Legal Tender: Women & the Secret Life of Money*, Christian McEwen skillfully weaves together true-life tales of wise and resourceful women as they speak candidly about their emotional connections to money. The stories are challenging, asking us to reassess our assumptions about other people's ideas about their finances. Some of the stories will stir your compassion while others will make you laugh out loud.

We need to talk more openly about how we view money and how our views affect us; this book opens a gateway to beginning that often-taboo conversation. In addition to the many moving stories, McEwen includes a thought-provoking list of discussion questions. *Legal Tender* would be a fascinating book to read with a book club.

—**CRYSTAL ARNOLD**, Money-Morphosis founder

Money was invented to facilitate the transfer of goods and services when bartering became difficult to manage. Since then, we have imbued it with all sorts of meanings that were never intended and wrapped it in multiple layers of secrecy and shame. Christian McEwen's book, *Legal Tender*, helps disentangle money from its shroud of mystery and confusion. Reading these stories is a healing process, and an invitation to tell money stories of our own.

—**MEGAN LEBOUTILLIER**, co-author of *Thin Places: Seeking the Courage to Live in a Divided World*

Christian McEwen has gathered an intimate—sometimes funny, sometimes sad—collection of interviews, focusing on women's relationship to money. It is clear that she created a deep sense of trust with each woman, enabling everyone to authentically share what was on their hearts and minds. Her book is a treasure trove of moving stories drawn from all walks of life.

—**JENNIFER LADD**, Money Coach and co-founder of Class Action